TRAVELLING WITH BIG BROTHER

TRAVELLING
with
BIG BROTHER

A Reporter's Junket Across China

SOLOMON ELUSOJI

The Question Marker
Lagos

Published in Nigeria by

The Question Marker, Lagos

ISBN: 9781089368755

Cover image by Ben Yido on Unsplash.
Cover design and layout by Ibukun Shobola

For my father, AY
who believed, to the point of tears

CONTENTS

Dedication   *v*

Epigraph   *ix*

Leaving   1

Settling   21

Hainan   47

Seeking Home   57

Hubei   73

Why are you staring at me?   81

Guangdong   95

Living   101

Shanghai   117

The People's Media   125

The Big Summit   137

Last days   143

Leaving, again   151

"This 21st century is the century for China to lead the world. And when you are leading the world, we want to be close behind you. When you are going to the moon, we don't want to be left behind."

– Nigeria's President Olusegun Obasanjo to China's President Hu Jintao in Abuja, April 2006

"For we do not wrestle against flesh and blood, but against principalities, against powers, against the rulers of the darkness of this age, against spiritual hosts of wickedness in the heavenly places."

– Saint Paul

LEAVING

Elizabeth,

*Y*ou described leaving for China as going to
war. I thought it was a funny metaphor. Now
I know it's true. It's like laughing at a joke hours
after one has heard it. Later you said I was becoming
Chinese. "Do people ask if you are mixed in China?"
I remember laughing so hard. Black boy like me. But
it also reminded me how little I had told you about
what I was actually doing there.

It all started with a phone call. I was lying in my
cramped apartment when I noticed the vibration.
It was the newspaper's Editor. The one I told you
about. Ms Nwogwugwu. For a moment, my mind
raced the clock and won. She never calls unless it's
important. And, as usual, she was brisk and direct.
She said she would like me to go on a training to
China, for ten months. Okay? Yes ma'am, I replied. I
didn't think, just said it. It wasn't until the call ended
that I realised what had happened. A bomb had been
dropped on my apartment and detonated. Nothing
was ever going to be the same again.

It was the first day of a new year. 2018. I had written IELTS the previous year and applied to British universities and received two unconditional admissions. Although I didn't have the money to pay the tuition fees, barely enough to cover my flight tickets and living expenses, I had also applied for a Chevening scholarship. So, 2018 was supposed to be the year I left Nigeria.

But not to China.

China was a land of factories and similar-looking people. It was a bland canvas, a place where people spoke in strange tongues. It was London in Orwell's 1984, where you can't use Google or Facebook. It was a dark, unknowable, distant land. Who goes to China? People who want to create knockoffs and manufacture cheap, low-quality goods en mass. So why would I want to go to China?

The question isn't a difficult one to answer. I just wanted to leave. Even if just for a while. At the time, as you already know, I was a newspaper contributor. It wasn't a paying position, but people and organisations paid to be written about and the line editors allowed my pieces to run, if it wasn't absurdly advertorial. I made enough money to rent an apartment on the fringes of a Lagos slum, buy food and beer. When I made some extra money, I tried to do some independent reporting. One morning, I woke up and travelled almost a thousand kilometres to Makurdi, to report on a devastating flooding. It was one of my proudest moments as a reporter, lodging in cheap motels for about four days and interviewing the victims, aid volunteers and government officials. I returned to Lagos with a bruised bank account balance, but it felt good. These brief spurts of ecstasy, however, couldn't hide the fact that I spent most of my time chasing public relations stories, after brown envelopes, after my own share of the national cake. It is quite possible to rationalise this behaviour but I felt my soul slipping away for every *truth* I chose not to include in a story. This sensation of *slipping away* manifested itself in various forms. I tried to fight back. Sometimes, *clients* asked me to send my account number and I would decline, even after the stories got published, because I wanted to be 'professional'. Of course I took money from others. It was an incongruous defence, a lukewarm, spill-out-of-my-mouth transgression. I couldn't figure how to balance the spiritual and the material.

So when Ms. Nwogwugwu called, I guessed that the universe was trying to help out.

★

One of the first things I did, in the wake of the

3

unexpected news, was to go in search of books about China. I found Peter Hessler, Evan Osnos, Ian Johnson, Richard McGregor. All white men. But I would expand my list later. As I started to clear the cobwebs, I was amazed about how much I didn't know about where I was heading to. A new world began to emerge right inside my apartment. It was almost like an epiphany, like being born again. I am Nigerian, but my education, my values, my identity has been shaped by the West. I read Western books, watch Hollywood, listen to American pop; I believe in democracy, in the idea that the individual is sacred. Maybe this is what it means to be Nigerian, after all the country is a British creation, a mere agglomeration of colonial interests.

So when I began to learn about China, it struck me that there was a different world somewhere, a reality that didn't necessarily correspond to mine, an alien matrix. I couldn't comprehend it at the time, of course. It was just a feeling, a sense of foreboding that made my soul leap. I was on the verge of discovering something. And I was eager to know what it was.

The travel application was pretty straightforward. My contact at the Chinese Embassy was Mr Fan, a bespectacled, charming diplomat whose first word to me was 'Congratulations'. He was in Abuja, so I e-mailed him the required documents. But I had to travel from Lagos to the capital city to get my passport stamped. The Chinese embassy paid for my flight tickets and I got a recommendation letter from Ms. Nwogwugwu to take with me. It was a generous recommendation, from an editor I had watched with awe in the newsroom arguing about the fine points of grammar late into the night. I am sure she couldn't even pick me out of a group photo, but she read my flailing, verbose and sometimes overly ambitious efforts at journalism and spotted promise.

After picking up my Chinese visa in Abuja, Mr Fan asked me to dinner, so I could meet the Nigerian journalist that had spent ten months in China the previous year. Bukola Ogunsina. I had reached out to her earlier. She told me, on the phone, that the training program was a fabulous opportunity to travel through China and expand my horizons. She intimated me about the stress of constant travelling and keeping up with what to write and the inclement weather, but her voice was suffused with excitement. She had had a terrific time.

When we met, over a banquet of Chinese dishes at a restaurant in Abuja, she turned out to be a graceful, kind woman. She practised her Mandarin with Mr Fan and his colleague and laughed as I struggled to wield the chopsticks. She gave me a few tips on surviving in China. But the one that stayed with me was: you have to act like an ambassador. When people look at you, they'll see Nigeria. So what you do matters. It was good stuff. But, throughout my time in China, I also came to realise that the opposite was true. It didn't matter what I did. Sometimes, what mattered was what my country had done.

In a twist of fate, I had also gotten admitted to study for a Masters degree in Global Journalism at Renmin University, as part of the training. More than two British universities had offered me admissions in the same area of study. But this was a fully funded admission. While studying journalism in the UK is not the same as doing it in China, as a senior colleague advised me, I quickly learnt that Renmin had the most reputable journalism faculty in communist China. That was something.

So I counted the days, while reading more books, articles about China. There was so much, too much, inundating. It was a bottomless pit.

I didn't pack a lot of clothes (didn't have much anyways); didn't pack any food, except a sack of garri and a handful of red, crushed pepper, which eventually saved me from a coroner's death-by-starvation report, during my early days in Beijing.

On the eve of my flight out of Nigeria, I packed my bags and travelled across Lagos to sleep over at my Father's. Together, accompanied by my sister, stepmother and cousin, we boarded a taxi to the airport the following morning. As I went through immigration, I was literally trembling, not with joy, but with something else. It was like being in a corridor that opened to heaven, a place you've heard so many good things about. And you are at the door, your hands on the handle, about to turn it down. Your heart is bursting at the seams with, what's the word now? Adrenaline? I don't know. But it was overwhelming.

When the plane took off and the map opposite indicated that we were out of Nigerian airspace, I felt lighter, freer. It was a moment of small triumph. Like many others before me, I had found a way to leave, too.

★

The first leg of the flight, from Lagos to Addis Ababa, was uneventful. But the second one wasn't. I sat beside a Chinese lady who taught in Africa and an Angolan scholarship student who had been to Macau. She was heading for vacation in China and he, the Angolan student, was resuming studies at a university in Beijing. It was a long journey and the company was great.

When the plane touched down at the Beijing

airport, I held my breath. My dog-eared copy of *Norton's Anthology of Fiction* was clasped between my knees, as the pilot steered us to a complete stop. The flight announcer demanded for Nigerian passengers to get off first. I fought through the already-crowded aisle. Behind me was another Nigerian, a teenager who moved like she had been here before. As we hurried through the tunnel-like extension that connected the plane to the first immigration checkpoint, she told me she was studying communications at a university in Beijing. She had completed a year of Chinese language training and was returning that spring to start taking degree courses.

She left me at the first immigration checkpoint, while I fished for my yellow card. I saw her far ahead on a later queue, at the last immigration checkpoint. I hadn't gotten the chance to collect her contact number. But she'd contact me months later, with a shocking surprise.

The immigration officer checked my passport and asked me to step aside. And I waited, for more than thirty minutes. While other black people joined me, some from Togo. We were eventually attended to at a police booth, where our pictures were taken before being allowed to proceed.

I found the airport stunning. The lights, the moving floors, the train shuttle, the smooth surfaces.

It was nothing like all the airports I had travelled through in Nigeria. This was something I would do frequently throughout my time in China: compare a piece of infrastructure with what I had experienced in Nigeria. It was my only terms of reference. And every time, the Chinese version, placed side-by-side with its Nigerian counterpart, was akin to magic. Once, I made a friend who told me Beijing infrastructure was one of the worst she had experienced in her travels across the world. I marked her off, in my head, as delusional.

Representatives of the China-Africa Press Centre, the training organisers, were waiting with a big sign at the arrival lobby. Some other African journalists had streamed out before I did. I ticked off my name on a list and went round, saying my name and country. There were journalists from Kenya, Zimbabwe, Botswana, South Africa, Mozambique, every corner of Africa. For the next ten months, I would travel across China with this group and make unforgettable memories. But on that cold February morning, we were complete strangers.

On the bus, I tried to keep awake and watch a foreign city for the first time. It was just past midnight. Skyscrapers rose against the night sky. The wide roads, the elaborate, intricate bridges, the almost saintly magnificence of the city. It was a lot to take in at once.

We were domiciled at the Diplomatic Residence Compound (DRC) in Jianguomen, situated at the very heart of Beijing. The DRC consists of a series of residential towers, tree-lined roads and guards swaddled in heavy coats and wool hats. During my time there, it was serene and secure. My apartment was commodious and well-furnished. When I had friends come over, I was always quick to remind them I wasn't paying the rent.

My first night, I could hardly sleep. I was brimming with ideas. My vision of China was already being reset. This was a *modern* city. And what about the apartment? It was one of the biggest and most comfortable I had ever lived in. So I sat down at the dining table (yeah, I had one, thank you) and wrote my first story from Beijing.

It was about *The Evolution of Big Brother.* Of course I had read about censorship and human rights abuses and inequality and environmental pollution and degradation, and all the other question marks hanging over modern China. But now that I was here, none of those things mattered or, perhaps, they mattered differently. And the article was exploring the idea that maybe the Chinese are right. Maybe a dictatorship, not a democracy, was the future of the human race.

The next morning, I went out looking for a proper

extension port for my phone charger. No one had told me that China's electric ports were different, two slanted lines running from each other. Walking down Guanghua Road, my hands tucked into my jacket, I passed a number of bars and embassies, including the United States consulate. But I didn't find an electric-appliance store. I turned into Ritan road. The farther I went, the more people I came across.

Along the sidewalk, people queued in front of shops, apparently for morning snacks. I found a shop selling a variety of things, including toys. But the attendant wasn't interested in my frantic gestures. I left, deflated. But, up ahead, I found another store. And this attendant spoke some English. She was excited to see me and asked where I was from. She also had the extension port I was looking for.

When I returned to the apartment, I stumbled on Omphi, my South African colleague in the elevator. She said she was having issues with her phone's Internet connection. I told her I could fix it and invited her to my apartment.

Omphi is fair-skinned and exudes a soothing intelligence formed through more than 14 years of professional journalism. She was one of the most critical, curious and honest minds I met in China. And she had a great smile, which appeared when I fixed her Internet connection problem, by installing a Virtual Private Network (VPN) application. I think I would be a very rich man now if I had charged a dollar for every VPN related issue I fixed in China.

Later, we had our first meal in the new country together at the Italian restaurant opposite our building. We shared a medium-sized pizza and two glasses of chocolate milk. It would be the beginning of a marvellous friendship.

★

Our first few days were about settling in. We received our first monthly living allowance (just over a $1,000), registered for a Chinese phone card, visited the hospital for a medical check-up and a nearby supermarket to shop for household items and groceries. It could have been overwhelming if we didn't have two Chinese assistants, Pinky and Marshall, to guide our every step.

One of my first biggest challenges was finding something to eat. The Italian restaurant served a lot of really great meals, but I soon got tired of asking for extra pepper. Together with Omphi, I tried a Chinese restaurant, which advertised itself as a great place for Peking duck. But when our order arrived, it was cold and sour. I almost threw up. So I started to finagle with my phone and soon found the Chinese McDonalds web app. Somehow, I managed to input my address in Chinese. When the delivery rider called, I would just mutter *dui dui dui*, which could translate to mean *yes, yes, yes*. And it worked. It would be a long time before I learnt enough Chinese to download the Meituan app and fully delve into the magic of food delivery in China; but with the McDonald's efficiency, I was beginning to get a glimpse.

One evening, during our first few days, I stood with some colleagues on the sidewalk, trying to flag down a taxi. But none stopped. It was windy and terribly cold. We bantered: perhaps the taxis were not stopping because we were black. At some point, I pulled out my phone and translated 'stop taxi' with Google. Then I screamed the phrase at the next taxi. To our surprise, the vehicle stopped. We ran towards it. Later, after acquiring a bank account, I started using Didi, the taxi-hailing app, and life just became a lot easier.

I also quickly learned that, in Beijing, cash was a burden. Whether it was at the big supermarkets or the petty trader selling used goods in the underground, all you had to do was retrieve your phone and scan the seller's Wechat or Alibaba QR code. As at 2018, the volume of mobile payments was the largest in the world, totalling more than US$ 12 trillion, from more than 700 million mobile users. And the numbers are not expected to slow down. Some analysts have predicted that by 2023, the country's annual total transaction value via mobile could reach $96.7 trillion.

And then there was the subway, which is one of the busiest subway systems in the world with nearly two billion rides a year. At first it seemed intimidating. I did several Google searches, inquiring how to pay and know when to get off. There was a lot of good stuff on Reddit. Descending the subway stairs, for the first time, I felt my heart pound. At the ticket counter, I held up my phone towards the counter to reveal my destination to the attendant. She understood and sold me the appropriate card. It ended up being pretty easy. The signs were in Chinese symbols and Latin letters. The announcer spoke, first in Chinese, and then in English. The train was on time. There weren't a lot of seats, but it was clean and airy and fast. The only thing I could think of, as I ascended out of the metro, was why Lagos didn't have one.

★

As I am sure you know already, meeting people from different countries gives you a feeling akin to spreading your wings across the universe. You feel like you are close to something truly universal. This was how I felt when I had dinner with Billy, who is Mongolian, Hafyza, who is Maldivian, and Tenga, from Namibia. Billy and Hafyza were part of the team of journalists from Southeast Asia who were also on a similar training program like ours, the Africans. We met at the Italian restaurant and talked about life in our different countries, about work, love and wine. Being selected for the training, it appeared, was also a defining moment for them.

I soon became close to Laetitia (Mauritius) and Ahlem (Tunisia), two of the most important people I met in China. They both spoke French but also enough English for me to, sometimes, interrupt their never-ending communion. My Kenyan colleague, Trix, became my de facto cousin, because she knew so much about Nollywood and Nigerian pop. We lived in the same building and, sometimes, when the writing was awry, I would appear at her doorstep and she would play some music and watch me dance drunkenly. And there was Tlotlo (Botswana), a magical adventurer, who always urged me to leave the apartment, leave the books and live. Go skydiving or hiking, she would say, do something different.

It was a thoroughly stunning education meeting these people. When someone asked me, some few weeks before I left China, what my biggest takeaway from the training was, I didn't think too deeply. It's the people I have met, I replied. To have friends from across Africa, especially, helped me think differently about the continent, about how we are all so different and yet so similar.

★

We had a bus. It was one of those long, tourist buses with enough space for up to 40 people. Our driver was Wang Bing, a chain-smoking, calm and dependable man in his forties. He didn't speak any English and his accent was too sloppy for me to even pick up the occasional phrase. But he was always early, ready to ferry us across the city, through traffic jams and toll booths. He was there, from beginning to end. And when he wasn't focused on the road ahead and lines formed across his brow, he had a disarming smile etched on his face

Our first official briefing was delivered by Mr Chen Zhe, the CAPC director whose English was a bit forced but kind. My English name is Alex, he said. But everyone I knew called him Mr Chen. When someone asked him whether we have to submit our stories to him for vetting before publication, he looked amused. We don't have such rights, he said.

The briefing was about getting us ready for the next ten months. The training was about helping us understand Chinese media, politics and society. And we were scheduled to attend conferences and summits, visit Chinese media houses and government ministries across the country; and also be treated to a staggering variety of Chinese culture tourism. In addition, we would receive a number of lectures at Renmin University, with guest lecturers from universities and think tanks across the country.

After the briefing, the group broke to head for our first lecture. Downstairs, I stumbled upon Hazem, the Egyptian journalist and asked him whether he was enjoying his stay in Beijing. He shook his head. I'm lonely, he told me. I mumbled something about how time will help him adjust better, but he looked disinterested.

Marshall, one of our assistants, sat beside me on the bus, making a phone call. When he dropped, he continued to tinker with the screen, his lean fingers dancing across the surface. Bespectacled, he was usually busy with his phone, focused intently on its machinations. I wanted to ask him how long it took for him to learn how to type in Chinese. The day before, while at the hospital conducting a physical examination, he had suggested that I focus only on learning how to speak and listen. It will be too difficult to learn how to write because of the characters, he said. So I wanted to ask him how long it had taken him. But, again, he was on the phone receiving a call. So I turned my face to the window and watched Chinese life in 3D: jacketed pedestrians standing at a zebra crossing, rows of bicycles parked on the sidewalk, sleek cars and giant billboards. I had never been to Europe, but I had read about London and Paris and the resplendence of Amsterdam. Beijing evoked those literary memories.

★

When I started to get some sleep, they came with nightmares. They all had a common theme: I would suddenly be back in Nigeria and then struggling to return to China, to return to this life where the electricity never blinked and water didn't stop running. I would wake and my heart would be thumping, beads of sweat on my forehead in the chill of winter. It wasn't difficult to understand what my subconscious was telling me.

The previous year, in 2017, I had interviewed a Nigerian who had embarked on the journey to Libya. Friday Eneji. He came to THISDAY headquarters in Lagos and said he wanted to tell his story. He removed his clothes to reveal the scars he had collected while trying to get into Europe. It was a difficult story to write, because I struggled to understand why someone would take the kind of risks he took, to leave. But, thousands of miles away from home, I was beginning to.

I was beginning to understand panic, desperation, but only a little bit. I still had no intention of staying back in China illegally. But that was because of the countless privileges (Oh Lord, these should be rights) I have had growing up, the parent that provided shelter, food and books, the public-subsidised secondary and university education I received, the newspaper internship that nurtured my journalism instincts. I could return and get a job and be relatively comfortable. This sort of privileges come with pride, the kind that protects you from the panic that pushes you to the edge.

But I don't believe the subconscious is subject to our hubris. At least mine wasn't. It was reminding me to do all it takes to remain *here*. You can't go back. You can't go back and not be able to return.

In a way, it was a warning.

SETTLING

*t*he first, and perhaps the most important Chinese political event we attended was The Two Sessions. We woke up early to catch the bus, which took us to the Great Hall of the People, where we joined the queue of journalists. It was always cold and windy. One morning, on the queue, we scampered off to look for shelter from the heavy gusts coming our way. The winter jackets were barely good enough.

The Two Sessions is China's stab at a democratic spirit, a conference of the country's legislative and consultative bodies, the National People's Congress (NPC) and the Chinese People's Political Consultative Conference (CPPCC), which includes popular figures like Yao Ming and Jackie Chan. The conference, a series of back-to-back meetings, usually last for about two weeks.

The NPC, made up of 3,000 delegates from across the country, is the country's legislature. But it is not your typical democratic law-making assembly - it has never voted down a proposed law from the Communist Party, China's sole ruling party. However, since it held its first meeting in 1954, instances of dissent and a lack of consensus have increased, leading some to believe that China is becoming increasingly democratic. In 1982, three delegates abstained from a vote for the first time. The first "no" vote was cast six years later. Then in 1992, only two-thirds of the congress voted in favour of the Three Gorges Dam, a highly controversial project that took decades to come to fruition.

Ordinary Chinese people do not elect the NPC delegates. Instead, they are elected, mostly, by provincial lawmakers who themselves are elected by lower-level assemblies at the city and county level. The public directly elects only delegates at the lowest level, which is the county level or equivalent. I found this spiral-of-hierarchy democracy interesting.

In 2018, discussions around the Two Sessions mostly revolved around a law removing term limits for Chinese presidents. The NPC also ratified a law to set up a new powerful anti-corruption agency and assented to the inclusion of Xi Jinping's political philosophy in the Chinese constitution. And, when the budget was announced, China's military spending was under the spotlight. But the Two Sessions was more than all these. There were also discussions around rethinking China's family planning policies, letting people with a foreign nationality keep their Chinese identity (China does not recognise dual nationality for its citizens. A Chinese citizen who acquires foreign citizenship will automatically lose Chinese citizenship), raising the individual income tax threshold, redrawing the central heating dividing line (in China only certain provinces are fitted with heating facilities) and raising Chinese university tuition fees, among others.

It was a time for Chinese leaders to come together under one roof and straighten out the country's most pressing issues.

I got access to most of the press conferences and meetings, but I didn't do any reporting. I had only been in Beijing for a few days and was still overwhelmed with the newness all around me, the language, the food, the skin colour. Our hosts gave us the feeling that this was a rare opportunity – to cover the Two Sessions was the dream of every Chinese journalist. But I wasn't Chinese and I struggled, at the time, to appreciate the significance of waking so early to queue in the cold and listen to speeches from Chinese leaders. At the press conferences, hundreds of journalists filled the room, jostling to ask questions. I raised my hand too. I didn't get picked, but some of my African colleagues got to ask questions. Later,

Omphi told me she suspected the question and answers sessions had been pre-programmed. I didn't think it was a plausible theory but, the next day, I read an article from a BBC journalist who wrote that "it is likely that reporters selected to ask a question have had it vetted by a government official who will coyly then say something like, 'Oh, let's hope you get to ask that'".

Meanwhile, I was flitting through foreign media reports, which were characteristically caustic about the conference's spirit. The BBC described it as China's "carefully choreographed political stage." The New York Times said it was "usually a sleepy, stolid affair."

And then there was Liang Xiangyi, the Chinese journalist who broke the internet when she rolled her eyes at a colleague's patronising question. Liang had been standing beside Zhang Huijun, from American Multimedia Television, who was putting forward a question to a Chinese official after one morning session of the NPC. Liang, obviously, wasn't impressed with Zhang's line of questioning as she rested her chin on her fist and then rolled her eyes, in front of TV cameras. Almost immediately, short videos and memes depicting the scene rolled out on Weibo, China's version of Twitter. "Nicely done! You gave an eye-roll on our behalf," one

<u>online commenter chirped</u>. "I am clapping for your honesty! Such questions are annoying and do not have any meaning," another said. But hours later, Liang's media accreditation to cover the NPC was revoked and her personal Weibo page disappeared, while search results of her name on China's social media platform were censored.

When I read the story, I showed it to some of my colleagues, who laughed. It was a funny story in its own way. But it was also a living metaphor for the foreign, mostly western, caricature of the Two Sessions as mere political theatre.

The Two Sessions reinforced what I had read about China, that China isn't a free-speech country, at least politically. The country is governed by the CPC, which extends its politics across every facet of society. Although there are other registered political parties, the CPC is essentially a dictatorship.

Dictators are not uncommon in the territory now known as China. For most of its history, it was ruled by emperors who wielded enormous, unquestionable authority. Some dynasties were great, others not so much. But the civilisation's core was held together by this system for centuries, perpetuating its culture and technology. It was the Chinese who invented gunpowder, paper, printing and the compass. Before the scientific revolution in

Europe, China was a superpower, a state confident, and rightly so, of its invincibility and uniqueness. From 1405 to 1431, buoyed by its large ships and superior naval technology, the Chinese undertook at least seven major naval expeditions to explore the waters of Indonesia and the Indian Ocean. Unlike the Europeans, the Chinese didn't travel primarily to trade or exploit wealth in other lands. Why should it? It had everything. "Our Celestial Empire possesses all things in prolific abundance and lacks no product within its own borders," a Chinese emperor, Qianglong, told the British in the 18th century.

So the expeditions, which reached parts of Africa, were designed to display the magnificence of China. They were "aimed to show the Chinese flag, bestow awareness and knowledge of the Celestial Kingdom on the barbarians, receive homage and tribute, and collect for the emperor those few rarities not available within its borders," David Landes writes in *The Wealth and Poverty of Nations*. "In particular, the ships brought back exotic zoological specimens - giraffes, zebras, ostriches, also jewels and potent animal, vegetable, and mineral substances to enrich the Chinese pharmacopeia."

But these expeditions, funded by the Chinese state, became too expensive. So the Chinese, content with what they had and who they were, retreated from the sea. By the middle of the 15th century, while the Portuguese, with their smaller ships were charting their route towards the wealth of the Indies, China, convinced in the completion of its civilisation, had given up on discovery. The government put in motion a closed-door policy that shielded China from foreign contamination. At some point, it was punishable by death to teach a foreigner Mandarin.

But China's isolation meant it was cut off from most of the industrial revolution happening in Europe and fuelled by resources from trading across the world. By the 19th century, Chinese technology had become inferior, outmoded, as compared to those possessed by their European counterparts. When the French and British went to war with imperial China, to gain access to markets and resources (as they did in the Americas, Africa and Asia), they were largely victorious. The Chinese couldn't compete. Then Japan, which was supposed to be a vassal of the Chinese empire, humiliated Beijing at the end of the 19th century.

At the dawn of the 20th century, China's imperial system, under the Qing Dynasty, was eventually brought down and Sun Yat-Sen led the formation of the Republic of China in 1912. But the country's political terrain was still fragmented, with conflicts between the Nationalists and the Communists, led by Mao Zedong. After years of civil war, the communists eventually succeeded in defeating the Nationalists, forcing the losers to flee to Taiwan. In 1949, Mao Zedong stood at Tiananmen Square and announced the New China, which was to be ruled by the CPC.

The CPC, initially, continued a version of China's closed-door policies, especially in relation to its past foreign oppressors in the West and Japan. But after a series of failed economic and social revolutions like the Cultural Revolution and the Great Leap Forward, a u-turn was inevitable. After Mao's death, the CPC, led by Deng Xiaoping, opened up China's economy in 1978, inviting wealthy western countries and Japan to invest in China and adopted liberal values in the management of capital. Although China didn't democratise its politics and still has a state-oriented approach to economic development, the country's economic growth, since 1978, has witnessed a stratospheric rise.

My initial thoughts, while attending the Two Sessions, was that China's one-party political system was responsible for its economic success, as it guaranteed stability. But other East Asian countries, like Japan and South Korea, who have had similar models of development to China, are have evolved into liberal democracies.

★

After the Berlin wall came down and the Soviet Union disintegrated, America and its allies proclaimed the end of history: the idea of individual liberty, that man is born free and has the power to decide his fate, had defeated communism's herd psychology. To assert this 'victory' and protect its national interests, America continued to invade other sovereign states, including Afghanistan and Iraq and Libya, on the pretext of vanquishing the despot and entrenching the divine values of democracy and the rule of law. While the catastrophic results of these interventions have been well documented, America's misty-eyed idealism caused it to predict that as China, a country rebuilding its economy after centuries of stagnation, became wealthier and grew its middle class, it was also going to become more democratic.

In 1989, a fierce uprising led by university students at Tiananmen Square in Beijing, called for democratic elections. The CPC sent the military to viciously quash the protests. The storm passed, but the protest has become one of the most visceral symbols of political discontent within China. Since then, the government has worked very hard in silencing politically motivated dissent, especially if it threatens the authority of the CPC's national leaders. Today, China is one of the most surveilled states in the world and the media, including the internet, is heavily censored.

The obvious question for me, while still taking in the magnificence of Beijing, was how much is freedom of speech worth? As a writer working in Lagos, I definitely had more creative freedom than I did in Beijing. But Lagos was no match for the infrastructure quality and standard of living in the Chinese capital city. So how much was my freedom worth, and did it really matter?

But, perhaps it was a wrong question to ask, because the implication would be that freedom of speech in Nigeria had stifled economic development, while in China its restriction has enabled progress. It's not that simple. A huge chunk of Nigerian history has been dominated by military rule, where freedom of speech was a crime. So based on the derivable equation from my question, Lagos, like Beijing, should have developed pretty much the same way. That's obviously not the case. But does that also mean that China's mode of restricting freedoms has not helped the country's political stability and, in extension, its economy? Of course that took me back to the long running debate on whether it is possible to build a great society without respect for human rights. But what is human rights if people cannot afford to eat, every Chinese official or policy expert I spoke to, hinted. By silencing 'troublemakers' the government has managed to focus on growing the nation's economy, lifting more than 700 million people out of poverty, since 1978. In other words, the end justifies the means?

However, whether the end really justifies the means or not, it is important to provide a little more context on how China became a communist state. As we have seen already, China declined as a world power through its self-imposed isolation. Its imperial system eventually collapsed under the Qing Dynasty in 1911 and Sun Yat-sen, a medical doctor turned politician, was declared the first President of the Republic of China. But it wasn't for long. The next year, he resigned for Yuan Shih-k'ai to take over.

Although the imperial system was already weak and unable to govern China's expansive territory, its formal end fully exposed the divisive nature of Chinese politics under the assault of Japan, which had vast imperialist ambitions and wanted to divvy up the country. Shih-k'ai, who ruled with an iron fist, attempted to re-establish the monarchy, with himself as emperor. But, too weak to resist Japanese aggression, he was overthrown in 1916 by some of his men. Shih-k'ai's usurpation led to the Warlord era when several armed groups controlled separate regions. Although the country was united by the Kuomintang (the Nationalists) in 1928, China remained weak against foreign aggression till the end of World War 2 in 1945, the year that marked the beginning of the Chinese civil war fought between the Nationalists and the Communists. By the end of the war, according to official Communist figures, about 1.5 million communist soldiers had been killed and wounded, 600,000 Nationalists troops were dead and approximately five million civilians had died as a result of combat, famine and disease. It was a broken, famished country.

However, the communists, who had come to power, partly through intense proselytisation in the rural hinterlands, knew their victory wasn't total. After all, the Nationalists had only fled to nearby Taiwan. So, to consolidate their wins, governing China would require an iron grip, a restless paranoia to plug every loophole and stamp to death any kind of dissent that could turn the tide.

I found this paranoia very much alive during my time in China. I found it in the obsession with mass surveillance. I found it in the sudden blankness of the TV in the DRC immediately CNN started to report on Taiwan or Xinjiang. I found it in a Chinese editor's strike off of the word 'expansionist' in an oped her magazine had paid me to write. I found it on my phone when trying to search for something on Google after forgetting to turn on the VPN. I found it in the silence (at best, reticence) of my Chinese friends, when I mentioned anything remotely political.

"We can't afford to lose the peace we currently enjoy now," one of them told me over a cup of coffee on June 4, when I asked why no one was talking about the Tiananmen square protests. And she said nothing more.

★

The first thing you notice is the queue outside the gates. It is estimated that more than 16 million people come here every year. Then you can begin to appreciate the separate halls and courtyards, the rooms filled with ancient artefacts. You might also feel a bit overwhelmed by the history, by the timelessness of the space and the power bubbling beneath your feet, buried for posterity.

Before we began the long hike across the high, steep stairs, our guide gave us translators and a map. Welcome to the Forbidden City, the palace of the Son of Heaven. But I soon put down the electronics, bored with the monotonous drawl of the voice in it.

The map too. It wasn't any use. I had my camera and my senses. And it was enough, to capture as much as I could.

We were visiting the Palace Museum, which once housed, for centuries, Chinese emperors. It was built in the 15th century by the Yongle emperor and was converted to a museum after the end of the monarchy in the 20th century. The names describing parts of the palace - Hall of Supreme Harmony, Palace of Heavenly Purity, Gate of Divine Might, Hall of Military Eminence - were high-sounding and flamboyant, metaphors for the Chinese worldview that the true Son of God used to live here, that China is the centre of the world.

This idea of pre-eminence is not something that is clearly visible in current Chinese political rhetoric. "Hide our capacities and bide our time," Deng Xiaoping said in the early 1990s. "Be good at maintaining a low profile. Never claim leadership." But if you look carefully enough, you will find it, both as echoes from the past and in the government's dizzying visions of the future.

During my time in China, I was more concerned about the past, about how we got here. The Chinese were too; actually they were obsessed with history, which is always carefully documented and consumed heavily by the public; a thing of pride.

One morning we set out for the National Museum. It was cold and raining, lightly. I had an umbrella, which I shared with Omphi. In front of the museum, while we queued under a sheltered space, a woman offered me a plastic bag for the umbrella. Then we went through a metal-detector and a thorough pat-down.

The lobby was expansive. The floors were neat; visitors milled around, curiosity lodged in their eyes. In Nigeria, as part of my freelance work, I had been to several museums, but nothing like this. Later, I would make a mental note, again, to stop comparing Chinese infrastructure with what obtained back home, but my brain kept doing it, contrasting, comparing, wondering what could have been.

One of the first things I spotted in the museum was a sculpture depicting the Red Army's major Generals during the Long March. It is 530cm wide and 220cm tall and made with reinforced glass plastics. It is easy to see the importance of the men. They stand tall, hands behind their backs, eyes to the future. Just slightly in front of the pack is the indisputable leader and eventual unifier of the communists during the Long March, Mao Zedong.

The Long March is the Communists' retreat during the prolonged war against the Nationalists. They were forced to travel for about 10,000km to escape being vanquished. Some estimates say they crossed 18 mountain ranges and 24 rivers to reach the northwestern province of Shaanxi. This brand of heroism appealed to many young Chinese and was part of the reasons many flocked to join the Party during the late 1930s and early 1940s, providing a template for the eventual defeat of the Nationalists.

We left the lobby and used the stairs to see the first – and what I believe to be the main – exhibition in the museum: *the Road to Rejuvenation*. It is a shout into the nation's history and dreams, a visual representation of what was, what is and what will be.

Official Chinese rhetoric tend to divide the country's history into three periods: a glorious past, decline and disgrace marked heavily by a closed-door policy which led to the harsh reality of the Opium wars, and the revolution and rejuvenation initiated by Mao's Communist Party.

The exhibition opened with a giant wall-oriented design by Tian Kuiyu that transports the visitor through time. The red-brown walls, probably made of clay, evoke traditional nostalgia, a sense of timeless craftsmanship that speaks to China's 5,000 years of history of making art. The details are bold, sometimes awkward, but they form sweet harmony. It is also replete with symbols, a conspicuous one being the Olympics sign which, although painted in brown, is unmistakable for its meaning: that China, in the beginning, was all that was.

Just immediately after Kuiyu's masterpiece comes artefacts and plaques that depicts the decline of Ancient China. 'The Lushun Massacre' by Li Wu and Li Fulai, a life-sized portrait of foreign armies mutilating ordinary Chinese, caught my eye. Li Xiangqun's 'The Chinese People Mired in Misery' too. The misery hangs in the room, heavy and true.

We used the stairs again, to the next floor of the exhibition, which addresses the struggle and awakening of the Chinese people, the moment when they sought to understand what had gone with their fabled civilisation. Then there is the revolution and reform and rejuvenation initiated by the Communist Party. It takes hours to take in this story, which is told through countless artefacts kept in pristine condition.

We left *The Road to Rejuvenation* exhibition and walked to a different wing of the museum to see *Friendly Exchanges Between the Witness of History*, which contained artworks bequeathed to China by leaders from other nations. There was the wood inlaid copper plaque presented to Mao by Cambodian Head of State Prince Norodom Sihanouk in December 1970; an Ebony wood female bust presented to Mao by Guinean President Ahmed Sekou Toure in September 1960 and countless more.

I went in search of art presented by Nigerian leaders. I found two. A Glass Sculpture of a leopard presented to Comrade Jiang Zemin by Nigerian President Olusegun Obasanjo in August 2001 and a Bronze Benin queen mother bust presented to Comrade Hu Jintao by Nigerian President Olusegun Obasanjo in 2004. They were in pristine condition.

I left the museum with a deeper appreciation of China's story. Of course, it had downplayed the deadly consequences of Mao's Great Leap Forward and the Cultural Revolution, but this is how nations are built, by chronicling a narrative of destined glory. It's not a matter of truth, but *your* truth. Yuval Noah Harari, the best-selling author and historian, said it best when he noted: "Movements seeking to change the world often begin by rewriting history, thereby enabling people to reimagine the future . . . they aim not to perpetuate the past, but rather to be liberated from it."

★

They called it the Silk Market. A multilevel complex that housed whole retail industries, from clothing to gaming to computers to jewelry. It was ensconced along Jianguomen road, a mere ten minutes walk from the DRC. And it was one of the first places I first went shopping for winter clothes.

Everyone, including the Chinese woman who handed me my visa-stamped passport, had advised me to pack thick, winter clothes. Although it was March and Spring was supposed to have diluted the cold, Beijing was stuck in single digit degrees. Some days it was negative. My 'Nigerian' winter jackets were hapless. I ended up ruining the unfortunate bedfellows in the washing machine, where I had turned on the dryer and shrank the material. Omphi and Tlotlo wouldn't stop laughing when I told them about the domestic accident. But the grave matter was that I was coatless and needed alternatives.

The Silk Market looked like a modern shopping mall where price-tags determined the value of goods. But it wasn't, mostly. The traders sat or stood in front of stalls and beckoned you to come in. The price tags didn't really matter. What mattered was how well you could haggle. One of the first Chinese phrases I learnt was *tai gui le* (too expensive), after I bought an overpriced coat. The sellers were persuasive - beautiful lady, they'll call out to my female colleagues, in heavily accented English. And they knew how to make a sale.

It wasn't long before we started looking for other markets. China was supposed to be the factory of the world where everything is cheap and in abundance. But the Silk Market, situated inside Beijing's Central

Business District, didn't reflect our expectations. It couldn't. It was like walking into a boutique in Victoria Island looking for the cheapest textiles in Lagos.

To find the cheaper markets, we took the subway. They were less cleaner and less fancier (the state of the toilet at one market, in Xidan, was revolting), but there we found cheaper bargains. I bought more jackets.

Once I opened a Chinese bank account, my bargain-hunting trips became a thing of the past. I had Peggy, one of our assistants, walk me through opening an account on Taobao and JD, two of China's largest online retailers. Back in Nigeria, I had bought things off Jumia and Konga intermittently. It was something I did out of curiosity or to feel cool, not because it made my life easier. But China changed my understanding of e-commerce. If I ordered something via JD in the morning, seven out of ten times, it got to me that same day. Taobao took three to five days. But the efficiency was stunning and I got hooked. I bought shoes, watches, shirts, a washing machine, phones, mostly for my colleagues. I became a mini online retailer. At times, my apartment would be littered with packages, which I had to sort and deliver to their individual owners.

At first, I had trouble dealing with the sellers and

deliverymen on the phone. They spoke Chinese and all I could say was *hao de*. But after a trial and error period (I lost some packages), I understood when to say *duibuqi, wo xianzai buzai jia, keyi mingtian huilai* (Sorry, I am not at home now, can you come tomorrow) and when to say *haode, wo lai le* and run down the stairs to pick up the package. Also, products could be easily returned and money refunded.

That year, Alibaba's Singles Day event became the biggest online-shopping day in history, firmly underlining the Chinese e-commerce market as the most dynamic and sophisticated in the world. The market's size has been influenced by the growth of mobile device ownership and internet penetration.

E-commerce is one of the sectors where developing China has managed to leapfrog those in the developed world. It has been described as one of China's four great modern inventions. Of course the Chinese didn't invent e-commerce, but they have used it as a tool of transformation, in unimaginable ways. In July 2018, the New Yorker magazine published a riveting story, written by the inimitable Jiayang Fan, about how e-commerce was upending life in rural China. Fan focused on JD.com, the Chinese online retailer reputed to be the third-largest tech company in the world in terms of revenue. The story opened with Xia Canjun, who grew up in rural China but rose to become a JD.com manager for more than two hundred villages, including his birthplace, where drones were delivering packages. China didn't need to adjust to mobile phones, Fan wrote, "because the country's wealth is too recent for people to have been swept up in the PC revolution, the way Americans were." So they were able to leapfrog developed countries, who had to struggle with the burden of non-mobile telephone infrastructure. In the same vein, Fan wrote, "people happily shop online because there haven't been Walmarts everywhere."

"In America, there's Walmart, there's Kmart," Jack Ma of Alibaba said in 2015 at a summit in Manila. "All retailers are everywhere so e-commerce is just like a dessert. In China, e-commerce is the main course."

Later, as my ten months in China wound down, we visited JD.com's campus in Beijing. It was a delight visiting one of the central sources of the phenomenon that had made my time in Beijing easier. We got a tour of the company's latest offerings, which includes an AI-powered shopping mall that has no need of cashiers; customers pick up products from a smart shelf and walk out, paying through a facial-recognition scanner at the door. JD, which started as a brick-and-mortar shop, was at the precipice of merging the online and offline shopping experience. The company was also investing in driverless robots and fully-automated warehouses. We also met with the company's Director of International Media Communications, Vic Gu, who stressed JD.com's focus on quality and authentic products and fast delivery across China. Mr Gu also noted that JD.com had its eye on the African market.

Meanwhile, it was not unusual that when someone heard I was in China, they asked what I was importing back to Nigeria. Electronics? Cars? Clothes? One of my friends back in Nigeria texted me and said she wanted to start importing human hair. How could I help? In the middle of the year, another friend suggested that I should start looking for how to go into 'business'. For a lot of Nigerians, this was the default picture of China - a place where it was possible to get the best bargains and become rich off the margins. The idea is not misplaced. In 2019, 25.1 percent of the total value of Nigeria's imports in the last quarter of 2018, calculated to reach N900 billion, came from China, according to the National Bureau of Statistics.

Nigerians have a huge presence in Guangzhou, one of China's busiest port cities. A lot of them are traders seeking to tame the ever swirling wind of profit. But there are also a number of undocumented immigrants, leading to a vicious crackdown by Chinese authorities. The Chinese say the undocumented are likelier to be involved in illegal activities like the drug trade, but there are real concerns that increasingly onerous visa renewal conditions have made it more difficult to stay documented. For example, Nigerians must submit criminal record checks for all work and student visas and, like other citizens of other African countries, they are not eligible for 72-hour or 144-hour transit visa exemptions. In January 2018, China's Xinhua News Agency reported that the African population, which is made up of a lot of Nigerians, in Guangzhou had decreased as "police have tightened enforcement on illegal immigration". There are now 15,000 Africans living in the city compared to 20,000 in 2009, but "the real number, including illegal immigrants and overstayers, is believed to have been much higher," the report said.

So when someone mentioned a business idea to me, my mind went to Guangzhou, which is more than 2,000 km away from Beijing. I wanted to go there and talk to the people there and write a story, not start a business. My bargain-huntings, throughout my time in China, didn't have any enterprise colourations. It was spent mostly on my phone, comparing prices of products in JD and Taobao and exploring other upstart options like Pinduoduo.

In late March, our first trip outside Beijing

was announced. But it was not to Guangzhou. We were heading to China's southernmost province, Hainan. I overheard that there was going to be a lot of beaches, so I joined a group of colleagues for a beachwear shopping spree at one of the many giant shopping complexes that dot Beijing. At Old Navy, I bought two pieces of light clothing. I gasped when I converted the money into naira. For the same price, I could have bought a wardrobe at Yaba market. But this was no time for bargains. We were leaving Beijing and its unfriendly cold, after all.

HAINAN

*W*e start to see the world in a different light as soon as we get off the *feiji* at Sanya's Phoneix International Airport. Although the sun can no more be seen, the air is warm, the skies are blue and clear. The group warms to this as jackets go off and smiles crowd out the twinge of winter. During the very short walk from the terminal to the bus park, I lose count of the number of relieved sighs.

What moves past us through the windows, as we drive towards the hotel, is an endless stream of picturesque hills, lakes and green fields. Then there is the South China Sea – blue waters that stretched the imagination eastwards, far beyond the horizon.

The hotel comes too quickly. It is a giant building with fat pillars, a sprawling lobby fitted with polished floors and a domed ceiling. Most of the rooms have a view of the ocean, which is separated from the building only by a brief thatch of green vegetation.

We have a quick buffet dinner – crabs, squids,

vegetables, roasted duck, rice, all sorts of things – and eight from the group wander past the green vegetation and towards the beach. It is dark. Distant skyscrapers glimmer in the distance. The waters charge towards us like a bull, then retreats. We step on it, into it, tease it. There is no music but that does not stop our dance. We shout into the void.

Walking along the beach, we encounter several couples dressed in wedding clothes taking photographs. The photographers have big cameras and those umbrella-like things professional photo-men carry around to help them control the vicissitudes of light. We also walk past men sitting on the sand, holding one end of a fishing hook.

The next morning, we are driven to another hotel in Sanya, MGM Grand, to attend the Boao Forum's Media Leaders Summit for Asia. I don't understand why this is important, or the geopolitics that necessitated its birth. After the Summit, we head back to the hotel, then lunch, before we are ushered out to meet with Sanya City officials and then have dinner with the Vice Mayor of the Sanya Municipal Government, Mr Wang Tieming.

Sanya on Hainan Island, China's southernmost province, is known as the Hawaii of China. In 2017, the city made the New York Times' top 52 places to visit in the world, where it was described as a destination with "stunning white sand beaches and shimmering blue waters."

In Sanya, the array of international hotels is stunning. St. Regis, MGM hotels and Hilton lie on a stretch of white-sand beach on Yalong Bay. Elsewhere in town, Hyatt, Westin, Shangri-La, Four Points by Sheraton, and other prominent chains have properties.

There is also no shortage of things to do, from water sports to taking a walk along the numerous nature parks that dot the city.

Once home to small time farmers and fishermen, Hainan's explosive growth has been largely fuelled by desire from China's central government to make it an international tourism destination. During the 1980s, the Chinese government designated the island as one of the country's "special economic zones", prompting property speculators to flock there. In December 2009, the State Council issued a memorandum that noted Hainan had been designated a "test case" in developing an "internationally competitive destination." In April 2018, President Xi Jinping announced that the government had decided to build the whole of Hainan Island into a pilot international free trade zone.

One method through which the government has pushed tourism in Hainan is through infrastructure development. A high-speed railway that zips around the island was completed in 2015 and the Sanya Airport is a stunning, modern edifice that facilitates flights between 136 domestic and 23 international airlines. The road network is also first class, allowing visitors move around hitch-free.

But, unlike a fairytale, Hainan's story is not without its problems. The Island has seen an astronomical rise in property prices, a phenomenon that has seen locals priced out of the market, leading to criticism from several quarters in China, including from editors of the People's Daily, a government-run newspaper. "How can we create a stable and harmonious living environment if the island's ordinary residents do not have the ability to buy housing?" the editors have written.

There is also the continuous battle with ecological deterioration, water pollution and construction chaos, problems which have been aggravated by the Province's exploding population. For example, population in Sanya city was 300,000 in 1988. By 2016, the figure had doubled.

Meanwhile, as more investments flow in, city officials are keen to attract more foreign visitors to Sanya. In 2015, tourist arrivals in Sanya neared 15 million, almost 70 per cent more than five years earlier and revenue from tourist businesses more than doubled over that time to $4.5 billion. But 98 percent of visitors to the island were Chinese.

★

The sun is up again, working its way from the east. It is our second morning in Sanya and we are on the bus, heading towards the Baopoling ecological restoration project. The scenery along the road is stunning; coconut trees splay lazily in the early light, green hills rear their heads across sloping landmarks and the road itself, shining like a polished shoe, snakes through tunnels.

Baopoling is a small town in Sanya that lies just off the G98 Hainan Expressway. The terrain is bumpy and surrounded by green mountains. The ecological restoration project we are visiting is a lush green mountain that sits just beside a cement factory. Mr Xing Yuting, an Environmental Engineer at the site, tells us that the mountain, which has been mined for decades for limestone, used to be bare, without any earth, until the government decided to restore it through a three-year project expected to gulp up to $20 million.

Already in its second year, the mountain's green mini-forest is evidence of remarkable progress.

While Mr Xing speaks and we listen under the

mild but bright sun at the foot of the mountain, irrigation pumps, which are powered by energy from solar panels, spray water across the massive hump. Several animals, Mr Xing explains, have also been transplanted into the ecosystem.

The mountain, after the three-year project, is expected to serve as a tourist site and is an indication of how governments in China, both central and regional, are focused on preserving the environment, Mr Xing tells us.

Later in the day, we are driven to Zhongliao Village, a model for poverty relief efforts in Sanya. China has set itself a target to eliminate poverty by 2020 and Zhongliao has emerged as one of the country's most fascinating successes. The village, which is about 18 kilometres from Sanya's city centre was, some few years back, just a small farming community. But, in October 2015, a project to renovate the village was launched. The aim was to build basic facilities for receiving tourists.

The project, which included the construction of a trail around the village lake, linking the village to nearby highways, and rezoning orchards and farms – was completed in early February 2016, just days before the Spring Festival, China's most widely celebrated festival.

That 2016 Spring Festival, the reborn village was

open to tourists "and visitors were welcomed by the lake and ponds brimming with blooming lotuses, rose gardens and various orchards, local fruits and food, as well as the characteristic hospitality of the Li ethnic people," China Daily's Zhao Shijun wrote.

Since then, tourists have flocked to Zhongliao to experience its beautiful, rustic magnificence, leading to the locals becoming richer as the need to open more catering facilities, inns, restaurants and cafes arose. Before the tourism initiative, the average local earned about 30,000 to 40,000 RMB per year. That figure has now more than tripled to between 120,000 and 150,000 RMB.

At the mouth of the village, community leaders welcome us with warm smiles. A set of battery powered, windowless but roofed cart-like vehicles ferry us into the community noiselessly. Villagers tending their stalls wave as our convoy sidles past. We stop at a bridge suspended over a river. A music performance by villagers standing on canoes ensues before we are ushered through a field of vegetables, where some of the locals are presently engaged, tending to the soil. On the farm, there is a tent that tourists can rent for a night. The space is neat and retrofitted with modern conveniences.

It is not difficult to understand why tourists come to Zhongliao. The village's natural design, tweaked by man, is simply refreshing. Away from the pollution that chokes China's large cities, for most Chinese, Zhongliao is Eden, a perfect garden transplanted from the beginning of time.

★

Our third morning in Sanya is spent at the Binglanggu tourist site, a commodious space packed with several historical and artistic museum-like spaces, a life-sized theatre set, restaurants, and multitudes of souvenir shops.

The first thing we do is to learn a new word, 'Bolong', which is a versatile form of goodwill greeting used by the locals, who are mainly from the Li ethnic group, one of China's most prominent minorities.

We spend several minutes at the museum-like spaces, admiring Chinese textile, woodcraft and clay art. One of the most fascinating artefacts on display is a vertically hung dragon quilt, which is described as the "largest dragon quilt of the Li nationality in the world." At 129cm wide, 284cm long and total area of 36,636 square centimetres, our guide tells us the fabric took several years to make.

Then we are treated to an hour-long folk theatre performance of the Li people featuring dance, music and drama. There is fire, water, wood, rice, boys and girls swaying to the rhythm of drums, tree climbing and love. One of the drama pieces is about a tradition where lovers demonstrate the intensity of their love through pinching. The more the pinch hurts the pinched, the more the pincher is believed to love. One of the actresses, fair and light, steps off the stage and begins to pinch people in the first row at the ears. When she reaches me, she stoops and then pinches, but it does not hurt.

Our last stop in Sanya is the Hainan Tropical Ocean University, where we meet with the school's officials and some of their African students. I scan curiously to find a Nigerian, since 'we' are purported to be 'everywhere', but there is none. I enquire from one of the School's Directors present at the meeting, Dr Wei Jing and she confirms they actually do not have a Nigerian. "But we welcome Nigerians," she tells me. "Tell them about us."

It's a new University, founded around 2006, but it already has a relatively large number of African students, mostly from Cape Verde and Comoros Island. The school's first African graduate is Waldir Soares, a six-plus-foot Cape Verdean who now teaches kids how to play basketball on the island and speaks with an American twang. When I ask him what he felt was the most amazing thing about Sanya, about Hainan, about China, he pauses for only a brief moment. "Safety," he tells me. "This country is really safe, man."

SEEKING HOME

i found out about Andy's Restaurant on the web. It was a Nigerian restaurant nestled inside Sanlitun Soho, one of the many sprawling malls that dot Beijing's landscape. One Friday afternoon, the sun dancing in the sky – welcoming spring's dawn – I slung my camera bag across my shoulder and set out. I used the subway, alighted at Dongsishitiao Station and walked ruler-straight along the edge of a busy road for about 18 minutes before spotting Sanlitun Soho ahead, a set of futuristic glass buildings that resembled alien domes. The area was crowded, not so much, but enough for me to squint nervously at my phone, trying to quickly decipher the GPS' directions before I get swept off into a black hole. I read numbers off the glass shops as I weaved through the giant structures, before spotting a plaque-like signpost that pointed me to the basement where Andy's Restaurant was hid, like a shy bride.

If I had not known that the Restaurant was Nigerian beforehand, I could have missed its uniqueness. The man at the front desk, which doubled as a bar, was Asian, and there were two other Asian ladies, servers perhaps, who looked towards my direction as I made my way in. I had to ask whether I was in the right place and the Asian man nodded, gesturing for me to take a seat.

The restaurant was designed to be deeply dark and mysterious. It was possible that the interior decorator that called the shots had wanted to recreate a vision of Nigeria as a bleak but beautiful country, a place where things were dead but hope flowed like a river. The tiles were black, thick black. The tables and seat were bold and brown. On the wall was a colourful drawing of a drummer working his magic and a dancer moving to the rhythm of the melody. The space was small, but it did not feel cramped.

I found a seat somewhere at the centre and the Asian man brought the menu. I asked him whether he was the manager, but he shook his head, muttered something in Chinese and disappeared. I returned to the menu, but before long, a new Asian lady, slender and tall, was by my side and she spoke English. I told her I was a Nigerian journalist who was curious about the restaurant's story. She was warm and had a small smile on her face. Andy was her husband, she said, but he was presently not around. I would have to wait till 22 hours. (The clocks had just struck fourteen) I told her that was not a problem. I had time.

Since I was not expecting the food to be spectacular, I ordered the safest option, for my palate, on the menu: egusi with okazi and pounded yam. When it came, the egusi looked white and bland. On my tongue, it was too soft. But these were minor conflicts. I rolled up my sleeves and dug in with relish, letting my mind wander, if just for a while, to a place I call home.

Halfway into the meal, a black man walked into the restaurant and proceeded to the bar, where he struck up a conversation with the restaurant's mistress. At some point, I thought I heard him address her as 'Nwannem', a word in Igbo that is used to address one's sister. Then, with a can of malt, a tin of milk and a glass cup, he walked past me to a table. And, as it is customary with most of the black people I had met in Beijing, he waved at me – this comrade in a foreign land, a smile forming across his fleshy lips. I waved back. He settled at a table just perpendicular to my right and, although his seat was facing the opposite direction, he refused to obey the geography of the arrangement and swivelled his body towards my direction. Which country are you from, he asked. I could tell that he was both amused and excited, but

I did not reply immediately: my mouth was filled with pieces of tasty goat meat.

When I finally did reply, he refused to believe. You don't sound Nigerian, he said. You should be proud of your country, now tell me which country you are from.

Now it was my turn to be amused. It is true that I do not speak with an accent, but I had not expected anyone to dis-Nigerianise me based on that. I was curious as to why he thought that way.

So I told him to allow me finish up with the food. When I did, I pushed the plates aside and invited him to join me at my table. Then I asked him why he thought I was deceiving him.

I meet a lot of black people who claim to be Nigerians when they are not, he said. I think you are from Sierra Leone or Liberia.

Or Ghana, I offered.

No, Ghana people don't travel, he replied.

Why is that?

Because Ghana is a very good country. Maybe after South Africa, Ghana is the best place to live in Africa. They have light and life is good. Why should they leave their country?

From here, the conversation moved towards familiar territory: politics. I have interviewed enough Nigerians to know that politics is perhaps the best conversation starter, the window through which you warm your way into their soul. And Sunny, the name my acquaintance gave me, was no different. He spoke with bitterness about the country's leadership and he did not tire.

Nigeria has money, he said, God has really blessed that country, but the problem is bad leadership.

When I asked him who he thought should be elected President in 2019, he was dismissive. No person you will put there that will make that country better, he said, what they need is for every state to be doing their own thing. If that is not possible, then they should divide into three.

I noticed, as we spoke, that Sunny spoke of Nigeria as something that he was not a part of, something that he had left behind. He used 'that' instead of 'we', used 'your' instead of 'my'.

Do you think dividing the country into three is feasible, I asked him.

Yes, he replied. Only three tribes make up the country: Igbo, Yoruba and Hausa.

But what about the Niger-Delta tribes, the middle belt, the multiple tribes spread across the northern region.

He shook his head. Look, there are only three tribes I know in Nigeria. The Calabars and Niger-Delta people are Igbos, they just changed the language. The same thing with Yorubas and Hausas . . .

I let him talk and explain, at length, his three-tribe theory without interruption. Before long, we were back to how bad the Nigerian leadership is. He was vicious with his condemnation, calling names and describing them with unprintable adjectives. I simply nodded and soaked it all in. It was quite obvious that there was a story beneath the rage, a personal story that had left him scarred, and I was keen to hear it. But Sunny was reluctant. Why should I share my story with you, he said, are you going to pay me for it?

Is this your first time in Beijing? I asked.

No, my first time here was in 2010, he replied.

He had been a trader, buying clothes and shoes from China and shipping them to Nigeria to resell. But in 2011, something tragic happened that made him stop. He would not say what it was, but he relentlessly cursed the Nigerian Customs for ruining him. When I asked him what he was currently doing in China (According to him, he had returned some two months ago before our meeting), he declined to answer.

I am not happy with what I am doing, he said. I am doing it with pains and I am not proud enough to say it.

What is it, I pressed.

No, I cannot tell you. It is not something that should be said.

Is it illegal?

Yes, but I am forced to do this because of the bad leadership in that country Nigeria.

He had grown up in Isuochi, a town in eastern Nigeria, he told me, and the local politicians had done nothing to develop the community. They did not do anything for us, he said. That place is still like bush till now. No light, no road. I don't know the essence of why these people travel abroad, because they are not learning anything. I am a family man. I have two kids and a wife in Nigeria. I am not supposed to be here. What am I doing here?

A stretched silence ensued at this point. I am fiddling with my notes, but my thoughts are jumbled up. This is familiar territory: interview subjects lamenting how the government is so terrible that they cannot but turn to crime. But what about personal responsibility? Still, the phrase – personal responsibility – is like gravel in my mouth, because I realise he is being held to a standard without considering the privilege of those, including people like me, who have set those standards. It was Ta-Nehisi Coates, in 'Between the World and Me' that wrote: "What is 'personal responsibility' in a country authored and sustained by a criminal irresponsibility."

Nigeria's criminal irresponsibility is well documented. The amount of money that has been siphoned corruptly from government coffers is so huge that it would not be an exaggeration to say that the entire economy is literally running on stolen funds. In 2016, a former National Security Adviser, Sambo Dasuki, was alleged to have diverted $2.1billion dollars that was originally meant for arms purchase for the fight against violent Islamic group, Boko Haram. When President Muhammadu Buhari shared this instance with Christiane Amanpour on CNN, she could hardly believe it. The former army chief, who had been voted the previous year on the platform of ridding the country of the corruption plague, had to reiterate his figure. Billion, not million dollars, he said.

When I finally found my voice, I asked Sunny whether he was going to return to Nigeria. He leered at me and then burst into raucous laughter. I don't want to go back anymore, he said, can't you see a beautiful China. You, do you want to go back?

I left Andy's earlier than I had anticipated. The sun was setting and the crowd outside was thinning. I checked my GPS and decided to walk back to the DRC, rather than take the subway. It would take an estimated 40 minutes, but maybe the evening breeze could help lighten the headache that had gripped me. Listening to Sunny had been difficult, because he confirmed the negative adjectives foreigners in Beijing use to describe Nigerians: the criminal, scam artist. I will, of course, argue that there are far more honest, hard working Nigerians than the dubious, but the stereotype is not exactly built on air. Once, I had visited Warri, an oil rich region in Southern Nigeria, and spoken to young men engaging in online scam. The justification was eerily similar to Sunny's: the government has failed us and we have to find our way. Once, an Indian colleague had asked me, what's wrong with black people? Nothing, I replied. We have just been unfortunate to have bad leaders. But he would have none of it. Other races, he said, have also had terrible leaders, but that has not stopped them from pushing the boundaries of progress. I saw his point and I threw my hands up. Then I really don't have an answer to your question, I told him. It occurred to me to talk about the Atlantic Slave Trade and the case for reparations, but, the way I see and feel it, the answer is multifaceted, a complex beast with many heads that can only be tamed with powers beyond my pay grade. Besides, I tried to console myself, a journalist's task is not to provide answers but ask the right questions.

The walking did help to clear my head. On the

six-lane Dongdaqiao road, which was heavy with traffic, I spotted some Asians taking photographs of cherry blossoms that had sprouted in the wake of spring. I brought out my phone too and clicked away.

★

The first Nigerian I met in Beijing was Yene, a student at Renda. She was studying for a Masters degree in Economics on a Chinese government scholarship. In the early days, I was always looking for Nigerians. I had this vague idea of writing a book about Nigerians living in China. It was Yene who assured me that Nigerians were available in abundance. Very soon, na you go tire sef, she said. We met, for the first time, at her dormitory. She cooked and offered me a plate of rice and hot stew. Then she added me to multiple Nigerian Student Groups on WeChat, while noting that she avoided most Nigerian groups.

"When I first came I was not like this," she said. "I was like you, always looking for Nigerians. I was very bored, lonely."

But the kind of Nigerians she met, at first, made her wary. One, who was apparently a PhD student, visited her once at her dormitory's cafe and, during their conversation, asked her where in Nigeria she hailed from. (Yene is Ibibio, from Akwa Ibom, your father's home state) The man then showed her his wedding ring and told her he had children back in Nigeria. But, since they were so far from home, could they start a sexual relationship? He was like "I have tasted Akwa Ibom women and I know they are very good," she told me. After that cafe meeting, she stopped responding to his calls and texts.

Salvation came in the form of church, where she met a number of Nigerians she was comfortable with. She invited me for a Sunday Service and introduced me to Itunu and Jummy and O'Jay and Nero, who had all come to China through Confucius Institute programs. I was excited to meet them and we exchanged contact details.

In April, Nigeria's legendary artist, TuFace, made an appearance in Beijing. At the concert, I met more Nigerians; students, business people, hangers-on. And together we danced to TuFace's rhythm.

I got to know about the concert when I visited the Nigerian embassy in Beijing. During the opening ceremony of the CAPC program, I had met a senior official at the embassy, who urged me to show up when I could. I asked him what he thought about the influx of Chinese loans into Nigeria and whether he had any concerns what would happen if we defaulted. He told me, frankly, that it would be great if the Chinese were able to buy off Nigeria and manage it.

Meanwhile, I never got to meet the ambassador, despite writing several letters and visiting the embassy a couple of times. He was almost always out of Beijing, back in Nigeria, apparently for political reasons. The word around was that he was a politician. I wondered whether ambassadors are also allowed to participate in partisan politics.

By the time President Muhammadu Buhari arrived Beijing in September, I had given up on the ambassador interview. Perhaps I wasn't tenacious enough. That was most likely the reason. And I wasn't tenacious because there were so many other things to do. But it would have been an interesting conversation to have.

But I did get to interview Charles Okeke, a Nigerian who had written a book calling for Nigeria to adopt a one-party system. Okeke studied Communication Arts at the University of Ibadan before taking up a journalism career in the early 2000s. But, in 2005, he travelled to China to seek better economic opportunities. By 2007, he had established his own shipping company and, subsequently, business was good. But he never forgot his intellectual roots.

"I left journalism but it didn't leave me," he told me the first time we met on the rooftop of the Bookworm café in Beijing's Sanlitun in the thick of summer. "I am still conscious of the things around me. It's like being a soldier. Even when you are retired, the skills stay with you."

In 2015, he decided to go back to school and enrolled at the University of International Business and Economics (UIBE) in Beijing to study for a Masters degree in International Relations.

"It's all about consciousness," he explained. "During all this time I was doing business and, to be honest, making money, I was never carried away. I always knew my future was in academia. Even when I discuss with people, they find it very difficult to believe I am a businessman because I don't talk like a typical one. So I always had that urge to go back to school. "

Currently a PhD student in China, Okeke's idea that African countries, Nigeria in particular, should consider adopting one-party systems was influenced, of course, by his time in China, Scandinavian socialism and the colossal failures of multi-party democracies across the continent.

"The case of Nigeria is not peculiar. The 55 African countries have the same problem. And it is that of leadership. Maybe Tanzania and Botswana are different, but it's mostly the same. This was designed by the colonialists. They left us with a democracy that is not democratic.

"It was a democracy that was badly constructed

and it has led to bad leadership. What that means is that it is a government of the elite; the trappings of power are such that you don't want to relinquish it. It comes with a lot of razzmatazz, in terms of finance and clout.

"So the problem with this democracy is that you should not have been elected using that method, because the method itself is flawed, skewed, crude. The democracy we have in Africa today is a faulty democracy. That is why we have to review it. By reviewing it, we have to have a democracy based on merit.

"If you look at the Nordic countries, it is very ironic that they have a monarchical system of government, which perhaps many of us do not know. And their kind of democracy is still such that the monarchy makes significant decisions and impact in their governance. After voting a Prime Minister, the monarchy still has to veto his appointment. Given that kind of scenario, I see it as a one-party state. Their system has been able to thrive, in terms of social democracy. Their tax system works. Tax is like a boomerang that funds social infrastructure and utilities. That's why these countries have free education at all levels, even up to PhD level. They have a functional and a working tax system. In Nigeria we don't have this. Apart from Norway that has oil, the others do not. They are leveraging on their capitalism to produce a socialist outcome."

It was a riveting interview that went on for hours. Later, I attended several meetings of the Conscious African Network (CAN), a group Okeke had founded for the purpose of "educating, enlightening and sensitizing fellow Africans, especially those living in China, on the need to get involved in the continent's rejuvenation. I told myself that there is the need to create a forum where we could begin to sensitize ourselves on the problem of Africa and where our young people can be engaged for change. The problem with young people is that they are always not interested in politics. But what they forget is that politics is always interested in them."

HUBEI

*t*he sun sparkles in its full glory as we leave the airport and travel across long bridges by bus, swishing past multitudes of lakes and rivers. Hubei has been described as a 'province of lakes' and its capital, Wuhan, as the 'City of Rivers'. If there was any doubt about the veracity of these 'aquatic tags', it soon disappeared as we reach the Yangtze River, Asia's longest and most powerful river. Today, the Yangtze is quiet, even tranquil; yet, as it ferries boats, large and small, it radiates an authority, a confidence that belongs to things that bristle with so much history, things that have seen so much change and yet survive.

"More than any other river in the world – more even than the Nile, which also cradles an entire country and nurtures a civilisation – the Yangtze is a mother-river," the travel writer, Simon Winchester, has written. "It is the symbolic heart of" China.

This part of the Yangtze River on which we are is

where it meets its largest tributary, the Han River and divides Wuhan into three towns: Wuchang, Hankou and Hanyang. We are leaving Hankou and crossing into Wuchang, which is the provincial government's seat. Wuchang, with its many skyscrapers and western-themed stores (McDonalds, Walmart, Pizza Hut, etc), is a city under perpetual construction, a notion brought alive by the ubiquity of cranes. Also, like Beijing, where I had lived for much of the past three months, there are rows of bicycles along the sidewalks and the road signs are written in white font, on blue background.

"My first impression is that this is a nice city, nicer than Beijing," my Egyptian colleague, Hazem Samir, says. "And that's because it is not crowded like Beijing and feels much more organised." Hassan is right. Although Wuhan is the most populous city in Central China, host to over ten million people, the ratio of its area size to population is higher than China's combustible capital. Here, too, the air appears to be cleaner, even if just by a fraction.

We check into the hotel – a Renaissance – and leave for lunch. Later in the day, we are driven to the Yellow Crane Tower. "If you come to Wuhan, you have to come here," our guide, a bright Chinese lady in a white shirt and dark slacks, tells us. The Yellow Crane Tower is what it is – a tower with five levels and roofs that jut out and point to the heavens like some kind of worship. It is the history of the tower, however, that pulls crowds to it. The tower is situated on 'Snake Hill' from where, legend has it, an immortal, Wang Zi'an, rode away on a yellow crane. Since it was built sometime in the second century, the tower has been destroyed more than 12 times. The current structure was completed in 1985.

At the fifth level, we stand at the balcony and watch Wuhan spread before us like butter on bread: a city made of blocks of apartment buildings, skyscrapers and, of course, the Yangtze. From here, the river takes a new shape as it crawls away, downstream, to Shanghai. In a certain way, it appears that the city was made for it.

The sun begins to set and we return to the hotel, where we are met by provincial officials who tell us about the strategic importance of Hubei in modern China, one which is built upon its unique location. And with shiny new ports, expansive and smooth highways, extraordinary ambitious airport and railway facilities, Hubei is doing a good job of connecting commerce within China and beyond.

The next morning, we set out for Wuhan East Lake High-Tech Development Zone (EDZ). The EDZ is one of the high technology development zones approved by China's State Council and has brought Wuhan global fame, especially in the area of optic-electronics and communication technology. At an exhibition centre in the zone, we are led into a cinema-esque space where we watch, from an elevated balcony, a 3D documentary of EDZ's story. Then we get a tour of the space, which is populated with cutting-edge technologies such as agricultural drones, biological cameras and innovative optic fibre products.

While China has largely built its prosperity on the back of specialized mass manufacturing and services usually involving technology imported from the west, Wuhan's EDZ is a potent sign of its ambition to become a much more sophisticated economy driven by the wheels of science and frenetic innovation.

We spend the following morning travelling to nearby Huanggang, where we visit a Poverty Alleviation project in Lijiawan village. These sort of projects, like the one we visited in Hainan, dot the Chinese landscape as the government accelerates its vision of eliminating poverty among its people. In Lijiawan, a village with 844 people and 234 households, the poverty alleviation project has resulted in a collectively built solar panel which generates power that is sold to the national grid. According to the village's Party Secretary, Zheng Xin, revenue generated from the solar panel's electricity each year go as high as 60,000 RMB (about $US 8,600).

Soon, we leave Wuhan via a high-speed rail for Yichang, the second largest city in Hubei, after the capital. Although Yichang, like all cities in China, also has its skyscrapers and large shopping centres, it is a much more sleepy city. It is however popular with tourists, majorly because it is home to the world's largest dam: the Three Gorges, a project that seeks to tame and harness the power of the Yangtze.

One bright, sunny morning, we set out on a bus to the dam. The roads, on each side, are flanked by mountainous forests covered with mist. Then there is the Yangtze, snaking through the terrain, tamed by the engineering marvel of man. We are driven to the tourist section of the facility, a kind of vantage point from where we watch the dam and the river it seeks to control. It is a gargantuan sight, something out of a Transformers playbook. And tourists, Chinese and foreigners, mill around, taking pictures with the dam as a background.

The Chinese ambition to tame the Yangtze river started sometime in 1919, but the country's many political and social issues did not provide enough stability for practical steps to be taken until the early 1990s. The two major reasons for damming the Yangtze, according to Chinese officials, was the need to fight flooding in the Yangtze basin and generate electricity. Critics however argued that such a project was bound to despoil the environment and displace millions of Chinese.

Sure, the project, after it went into operation in the 2000s, did displace a lot of people, but the government said it provided relocation facilities and funds for those affected. In 2017, flood control authorities in China also noted that the Three Gorges had played a big role in relieving flood pressure downstream. Also, the Three Gorges, which cost almost $28 billion to build, is the largest hydroelectric gravity dam in the world, with an installed capacity of 22,500MW.

Well past noon into the visit to the Three Gorges, I found myself watching the river from across a rail as men, at the banks below, threw hooks into the water, looking for a catch. The river's surface had a light-brownish hue as it danced nonchalantly away, unamused. I wondered about the depth and might of the stories it bore, from Tibet to Shanghai. But my thoughts did not get very far. I had read about the river, but I did not know it. Its tale was transmitted in a language alien to my ears.

The last dinner in Yichang was eaten with local officials. There, I started a conversation with a local foreign ministry official who had grown up in the city. "Yichang was a much more quiet city," he told me. Then the Three Gorges came and brought with it a lot of development. "It is still a quiet city," the official said. "It is not a busy place like Shanghai or Beijing. It is the sort of place where you come to after retirement and enjoy life." He did not say as much, but I saw that he was proud of what his city had become. Last April, the Chinese President, Xi Jinping, had visited Yichang, to inspect some environmental restoration work along the Yangtze. It was the first time, in many years, a sitting President had showed up. "That was a very proud moment for us," the man said.

WHY ARE YOU STARING AT ME?

*i*t happened in Wuhan, where we saw the Yellow Crane Tower. Omphi and Tlotlo said they had been racially profiled. On our first night at the hotel, they had gone downstairs to the pool. But immediately they dipped into the water, two Chinese women hastened to get out.

Being a black person in China comes with a lot of baggage. From the moment I stepped off the plane, this was obvious, from the countless eyes that tracked my movements to strangers who unabashedly point their phones and click away. And then the ones who ask to pose with you in trains, supermarkets, on the streets. I found most of it comical. It was new, this idea that my skin was exotic. Once, I went to the Wangfujing bookshop to buy English titles and the old lady who collected my cash notes, held my hand briefly, rubbing the back of my palm and looking up in wonder when she realized the skin wasn't going to peel off. I found it funny. I thought she was strange and curious, not racist.

But my Southern African colleagues felt such behaviour were incontrovertible proofs of racism. It got me thinking about what it meant to be racist. I started to interview every black person I could find in China. Hey, would you describe Chinese people as racists? Some of the responses I got were interesting. Asithandile Thando Ntsokota, a South African school teacher, told me:

> *I knew that there is a lot of racism here. But I don't want to focus on that. Racism here is not in my face. It's just subtle. That's the way I've experienced it. Most people are friendly to me. But I have never had it in my face. For example, they prefer Europeans as English teacher, without considering the level of proficiency. I remember going to school for an interview. They said they only wanted native speakers. But I met one of the teachers. She was Russian. When we spoke, she had a very deep Russian accent. And her grammar was not good. But she was working there already. So when you are black in China, you need to prove yourself more. It's how things work in China. If you are white, you are right. But as a black person, if you always look for racism, you are going to see it. If you do that, you will be stressed. So I just don't pay attention. I just*

do my job. I don't want to stress myself, because racism is everywhere in China. Fighting racism in China, I will never win. I am a foreigner. But in conversations, I try to talk proudly about black people. We are smart and not inferior.

Scell Atiley, a Ghanaian student, said:

I have experienced a lot of racism here, but I overlook it. I guess it's just something normal, since black people here are a minority. Even if It's getting better, people still want to touch your hair and ask lots of questions like why are you so dark? Why is your skin like that?

Honestly, this is the only challenge with Africa and China relations, the racism. I feel we should see each other as one people, as human.

At a Think Tank conference in Beijing, I posed the question to Dr. Hodan Osman, a Somali academic who teaches in a Chinese university. She said it was misleading to describe Chinese as racists. The appropriate frames, she suggested, would be constructed out of words like curiosity and ignorance. But was she simply being diplomatic? After all, she had spent most of her academic career in China, as a student and professor, and was a shining symbol of

China's smooth integration with Africa.

In 2017, Dr Osman was interviewed by the BBC. They asked her if China's recent activities in Africa could be described and equated with western colonialism. She was visibly appalled by the suggestion. "I can never understand how anyone can bring it to comparison," she said, speaking in fluent mandarin. "It is difficult to imagine. What did the colonists do in Africa? They treated humans worse than animals are treated, took people out of the continent and enslaved them." So "how can the term colonialism, and historical meaning the word entails, be used to describe the current relationship between China and Africa? I think it is extremely obtuse."

I understood Dr Osman's line of thought. But she was speaking from a government policy perspective. From its acclaimed non-interference approach to international relations and flexible approach of engagement in Africa, bereft of ideology, the Chinese government is perhaps the continent's least racist partners. "What they want to help you with, is what you have identified as your need," former Sierra Leonean Minister of Foreign Affairs, Alhaji Momodu Koroma, says. "With Britain, America, they identify your needs. They say: "Look, we think there is a need here." And China is also known for the elaborate manner in which it dignifies government officials from Africa, irrespective of the size of the countries. "There's something about how the Chinese government treats an African delegation, regardless of how small or weak the country is," a former Liberian Minister, Gyude Moore, says.

But government policy is not the same thing as the day-to-day experience of a black person living in China, which is where the racism lives. Sometimes, it spills over into the media too. In February 2018, a few days before I arrived China, a comedy skit designed to celebrate Sino-African ties on one of China's biggest TV shows featured an Asian actress in blackface with exaggerated buttocks. The incident sparked widespread accusations of racism. When we met Chinese officials working in culture and media and Omphi repeatedly tried to get clarity on what's being done to prevent a repeat occurrence, the responses were usually vague. Since the Chinese maintain they are friends to Africa, they believe it is impossible for Chinese people to be racist and, subsequently, blame western media for trying to stoke crisis in Sino-African ties.

It is also possible that Chinese unfamiliarity with the black skin has little to do with ignorance than repulsion. Frank Dikotter, in *The Discourse of Race in Modern China,* notes that: "In contrast to racial thinkers in Europe and the United States, writers in China rarely made analogies between humans and apes. But they did not hesitate to point out that Africans were at the bottom of the social hierarchy. Since ancient times in China, blackness was the mark of the slave."

It was the Communist Party, led by Mao, which began to extend a hand of fellowship towards Africa, based on a shared struggle against white colonialism. But Dikkoter points out that the propaganda was based on 'class struggle' not racial equality:

In its propaganda about revolution, China placed itself on the top of a global racial hierarchy, leading the 'coloured peoples' on the bottom towards liberation. This was apparent in Africa, where China tried to capitalise on a common racial identity, urging that 'we blacks stick together' against the 'white race', an idea which was met with scepticism on the African side. Acting troupes endeavoured to propagate the idea of racial solidarity, as was exemplified by a play performed in Rwanda in the early 1960s: A tableau depicted a black man sitting on a throne; a Chinese actor with a white mask then entered and knocked him off [groans from crowd]. A Chinese with no mask entered, knocks the 'white man' in turn off the throne, picks up the African from the ground and helps him back on to the throne [cheers from crowd].' . . Despite the communist imagery of racial unity with the victims of imperialism, many Chinese adopted an aloof and exclusive attitude during their stay in Africa. Africans studying in China, on the other hand, were often the victim of indirect or overt discrimination. Emmanuel Hevi, a Ghanaian studying medicine in Beijing in the early 1960s, testified to the continuous discrimination Africans had to endure in China. He perceived paternalism as an important form of prejudice: 'In all their dealings with us the Chinese behaved as if they were dealing with people from whom normal intelligence could not be expected.' As Michael Sullivan has pointed out, Mao's assistance to Africa reinforced the negative image of Africans as passive recipients of the fruits of higher civilisations, and intensified popular discontent at wasting wealth on Africans when many Chinese lived in extreme poverty.

Dikotter went on to state that little has changed:

Attitudes have not improved in the twenty-first century. M. Dujon Johnson calls it 'Afrophobia', noting how 'In China today there is a clear social hierarchy based on the assumption of racial superiority' . . . It is a sad indictment of how little racism has changed over the past twenty years that the only prominent scholar in China who actually studied the phenomenon and denounced it publicly, namely Liu Xiaobo, (died in 2017) is now lingering in gaol. It was still possible, twenty years ago, to imagine that the racism that could then be found in the People's Republic was merely the result of ignorance after the country had been closed to the rest of the world for decades under Chairman Mao. Denial, rather than ignorance, appears to be the norm today.

Before the Wuhan incident, I wouldn't have described what I experienced in China as racism, because my conception of the idea, like Dr Osman's, was steeped in the Atlantic slave trade and colonialism, mostly products of rabid western imperialism, of insatiable greed. But after mulling over Omphi and Tlotlo's experience, I realised it was foolish not to call what is described as Chinese 'curiosity' or 'ignorance' for what it really is: racism. To say otherwise is to sugarcoat it, to ridicule the black experience, to ask for understanding while the trampling continues. To say otherwise is to be complicit in the degradation.

Ending racism in China will be difficult. Since

the country doesn't have a history of black slavery and colonialism (at least nowhere near the scale associated with Europe and America), it doesn't suffer the curse of guilt. Most black people in China are willful immigrants chasing a better life. So, as I found out in my interview series, the discrimination is something they are ready to put up with and justify, even if they call it for what it is. "I have come to understand that their racism is just due to ignorance," Kehinde Awosusi, a Nigerian Masters student in Beijing, told me.

Also, as we have seen through Dikotter, Africa's economic dependence on China can fuel racial sentiments. The predominant narrative in Chinese media is how a powerful China is lending a helping hand to Africa. It is not a lie. But it downplays, heavily, the fact that China's gifts are not essentially free. "African people have so many opportunities when they come to China," one of my Chinese friends told me, when she heard about my Masters degree at Renmin and how I had got in. "But as a Chinese person, everything is so competitive. It is not fair." These sort of sentiments, short sighted and fallacious as they are, contribute to the idea that the Africans are free-riders who have little or no economic value to Beijing's ultimate interests. And this is the genesis of all racism: when a certain group believes the other has no inherent commensurate value or worth, compared to themselves.

★

To acknowledge Chinese racism isn't to deny Chinese friendship. Despite my general outlook of race in China, I made a lot of Chinese friends while living in Beijing; friends whose memories stayed with me long after I had left the country. One remarkable individual was Heather Li, who swears she has African roots. Light-skinned and petite, she doesn't have the genetic evidence to prove it, but her claim isn't based on biology.

In early 2019 during the Chinese New Year, Li visited Africa for the first time to "find her roots", when she travelled to Nairobi, Kenya. Before the trip, she painted her nails the colour of the Kenyan flag and posted on WeChat, "this girl is Kenyan-READY!" When she eventually landed at the Nairobi airport, she posted, "Heather's finally home."

"My trip to Kenya was amazing," she told me later. "I really didn't feel like I was visiting there for the first time. Sometimes you go to a new place and you feel lost. But in Kenya, I connected with so many people I hadn't met before. It felt like home. I just wished it was longer, because I didn't experience everything."

In Kenya, Li adopted Kenyan parents and got an African name, Makena Akinyi. Makena, which is from the Meru tribe means 'happiness' and Akinyi, from the Luo tribe, means 'born in the morning'. She also visited safari parks and got to pat the skin of baby elephants. She took a tour of traditional Kenyan homes. In one picture posted on Wechat, a Chinese chat app, she can be seen posing in front of a hut tagged '1st wife hut'. "Most (definitely) first wife material right here," she captioned jokingly.

Li didn't grow up to love Africa. She grew up in Beijing in what she described, to me, as a singular culture. "I didn't have access to the international community," she said. But she went to college in the United States and her outlook changed. "When I was growing up, I never thought I was Chinese or paid attention to my skin tone, until I went to America," she told me. There, she decided that she "wanted to be a bridge between China and different cultures." She chose to identify with African cultures.

Of course, a Chinese claiming to be from Africa is obviously bound to raise eyebrows and questions about cultural appropriation. "I am very conscious about it," she said. "Sometimes, I do feel like people are giving me side-eyes, like some Africans are thinking 'what is this girl doing?' It's awkward. It's easy when my friends tell me. But for someone who doesn't know me, it might be hard. But it's just natural for me. Everytime I talk about Africa, I am happy.

"Of course, I need to educate myself more, about the history, the culture, read more stories. I should dig in more if this is something I am connected to. I am always learning, but there is still so much to learn. I feel people shouldn't just label others. The intention is the most important thing."

Li believes the biggest threat to China-Africa relationship is that "there's not enough mutual understanding due to stereotypes and generalisations.

"I think we should work together more, instead of assuming the worst. I would really love China and Africa co-producing films and telling their stories. So that people can see the reality. People who live in China and Africa live a different lifestyle than what's on television."

When I asked her about racism in China, she said: "Racism is a hard topic to discuss. I think racism is everywhere and people like to put people in a box. Most times, in China it's just ignorance or the fact that Chinese people haven't got used to having other cultures around. Sometimes I feel like my African friends take offense when Chinese people are just curious.

"But I also have to think as a black person (even

if I would never know how it's like to see the world as a black person). How would I feel if people stare at me and take pictures of me? I won't feel comfortable.

"I think empathy is important. We should have more spaces where we put people together and they can learn about one another. I believe those spaces are important."

GUANGDONG

*t*he Dragon Boat festival was marked in June. There were no dragons on the street, but we attended a cultural event where we made zongzi, a form of Chinese rice dumplings wrapped in banana leaves with a pyramid shape. One of my Chinese friends, Sally, also gifted me wraps of zongzi, which I couldn't manage to eat. Splashed in the front pages of China Daily were pictures of dragon boat racing and a feature on how foreigners in China marked the festival - a lot of the answers had to do with making and eating and being gifted rice dumplings.

On June 19, we departed for Guangdong Province, one of the most important economic centres in China. We were scheduled to visit Shenzhen, Zhuhai and Guangzhou. Each of these cities are economic powerhouses, prominent pillars of China's renaissance. According to state statistics, Guangdong's GDP in 2017 reached $1.4 trillion. Nigeria's GDP in 2017 was $375.8 billion.

We landed in Shenzhen in early afternoon. The airport was close to a body of water. Shenzhen was formerly a poor fishing village before it was designated as one of China's initial special economic zones, an experiment that pulled in capital from across the world and transformed the country. From the airport, I marvelled at the futuristic shape of the city's infrastructure: the well-manicured roads marshalled by green trees at both ends, the tall buildings that crowded the city centre.

Our first stop was the Shenzhen Museum, which was then displaying a 'Reform and Opening up' exhibition. Then we visited the Huawei campus where we got a tour of product showrooms while interfacing with some of the company's international executives. The next morning, we visited DJI's campus, where we got the chance to operate drones with hand motions. The technology wasn't perfect, but it was fascinating. From DJI we headed to Hytera, a radio communications company that has clients across the world. The last company we toured in Shenzhen was BYD, an automaker with global ambitions.

Later that afternoon, we left Shenzhen for Zhuhai, which turned out to be one of the most fascinating bus-trips I took throughout my stay in China. For more than 150km, as we traversed past lush lakes and damp fields of rice, I didn't spot an odd bump or pothole. In disbelief, I leaned backward and tapped Trix. Are you sure this is not a public relations bubble? How is this even possible? They definitely built this to impress a couple of African journalists. She chuckled at my conspiracy theories and put back her earphones.

We saw Zhuhai before entering it. From a distance, the city was bathed in light, casting off dusk's gloom. Like Lagos, it was surrounded by a large body of water. But while most of Lagos's aquatic splendour is bare and despoiled, even nauseating, Zhuhai's was resplendent, harbouring hotels and shimmering with glamour. At the hotel lobby, I started a conversation with one of the managers, Merry, a migrant worker who had just returned from the UAE. Even after we left Zhuhai, we kept in touch. She later went to Macao, to work in another establishment.

We were in Zhuhai, primarily, to tour the world's longest sea bridge, which links Hong Kong and Macao to the Chinese mainland, and meet with local government officials. The bridge, which would officially open some months later, is 55km long and, similar to mega projects like the Three Gorges Dam, another symbol of the Chinese government's determination to bend the forces of nature to its will. Estimated to have cost $20 billion, construction began in 2009. But the project delivery date of 2016 had to be pushed forward due to construction delays, budget overruns and safety issues. Nine workers died during construction and 200 others were injured. In 2018, six subcontractors were fined for endangering workers.

That morning, while we were being driven across an empty bridge, the sea stretching interminably at every side, I wondered, like I did for most of my time in the country, at the engineering marvel the project was. At a point, the bridge disappeared into the water, through a 6.7km undersea tunnel that had been added to avoid disrupting shipping lanes. The tunnel was connected by two artificial islands, built because of the bridge. It was set to become a tourist attraction. One month after it opened, a Hong Kong tourism official said perhaps 20 percent of the passengers who had used the bridge had just come to "worship the bridge". They had no intention of entering Hong Kong.

Later that afternoon, after having lunch with local government officials on one of the artificial islands, we set off for Guangzhou, one of China's most famous port cities.

Guangzhou's streets were narrower than most Chinese cities I had been, including the street on which our hotel was situated. The air reeked with commerce and there were more black people on the sidewalk than anywhere we had been in China.

A lot of my colleagues had been looking forward to shopping for cheap goods in the city and after dinner, I joined a group to wander the back streets. The market was rowdy and chaotic and sellers encouraged hardcore bargaining with their initial astronomic prices. While my colleagues picked up shoes and dresses, I decided to return to the hotel. The story idea circling in my head had to do with the experience of African traders in the city, and there were none in the market we had stumbled into.

The following morning, through a heavy downpour, we visited the Guangzhou University of Chinese Medicine, which contained ceiling-high shelves stocked with transparent medicine jars. Inside the jars were an assorted range of herbal ingredients, including snake blood. Later, we visited an African Community where we were handed city brochures and pamphlets. We met the officials in the evening, where questions regarding the influx of cheap goods from China to Africa were raised. The city officials didn't deny the charge but shifted much of the blame on dishonest African traders who collude with sub-par Chinese manufacturers. We can't inspect all the goods that go out of Guangzhou, the official said.

The next morning, we flew back to Beijing. I

didn't have my story. I knew I would have to go back
to get it.

LIVING

*b*y June, Beijing had gotten warmer. Summer was ready for an overtake. And I had also resolved to improve my Chinese. The Beijing International Chinese College's (BICC) job was to introduce us to the language. But to learn a language is to also learn its culture and history. So the college facilitated a variety of cultural activities, slowly immersing us into what it means to be Chinese. We visited cultural centres and attended acrobatic shows, teahouse performances, and festival celebrations. In early April, we attended a Qing Ming festival show, where we wore Chinese robes and adorned our heads with crowns made of leaves.

We spent a lot of time at the college's Maquanying campus, sited in a quiet suburb of Beijing with two-lane roads, modest buildings and, sometimes, the din of ongoing construction. It was where we had our first Chinese lessons. It was also where we first came across Gu Zheng, a traditional music instrument, built around the strumming of chords. The artiste sat in the middle of a quiet hall and made music about nature, mountains, seas, about the elements that have forged human history.

At BICC, we were split into three classes. The teacher for my class was Mr Hao, a slim, young Chinese who liked to run his hand through his tousled hair. He was patient and disciplined and helped us through the fundamental basics of the language. I downloaded Duolinguo, an app I had used half-heartedly to improve my French years ago. I also convinced a Nigerian friend, who was studying Chinese, to give me some lessons.

Chinese languages have a rich, variegated history that stretches across thousands of years. The modern dialects are written in similar characters but their speakers do not understand one another. For example, a Hakka speaker can't naturally understand Cantonese. The version I started to learn in China, Modern Standard Chinese, is based on the Mandarin dialect. In 1956, the government decided to make the language more accessible by introducing a new system of romanization called Pinyin.

In 2004, the first Confucius Institute appeared in Seoul, South Korea. The Institute's stated goal is to promote language and culture, support local Chinese teaching internationally, and facilitate exchanges.

Like the UK's British Council, France's Alliance Francaise and Germany's Goethe-Institute, it was another sign that China was ready to embrace the world, in a bear hug. As of December 2017, there were 525 Confucius Institutes and 1,113 Confucius Classrooms in 146 countries and territories around the world. At least three are in Nigeria.

The growing allure of Chinese, also, is closely related to China's growing economic profile. More and more people are travelling to China for university degrees and dealing with Chinese businesses. But Chinese characters, which number up to 50,000, make the language difficult to learn.

I started to learn the characters on my own; I filled up notebooks and purchased flash cards and wrote and rewrote hundreds of characters. But, for months, it seemed I was making no headway. I blamed the DRC's isolation and the bloody characters and the tones and my memory. But, to my credit, I didn't relent. I kept at it, tinkering with Duolingo's gaming approaching and making foolhardy attempts at transcribing the subtitles of a Chinese feature film. Like most adult beginners, I tried to impose one language's common sense rules on the other, but I quickly retraced my steps. It also helped that I was bilingual, so I could understand, much faster, the idea that a language creates its own universe.

I wanted to learn Chinese because I wanted to understand China. It never occured to me that I could write about the country with any depth, if I didn't understand its tongue, the code with which it translates the invisible to reality. But I was also fascinated with how central the language was to the country's identity. There were English translations on the subway and road-signs written in roman scripts. But Chinese characters were clearly pre-eminent. And when political leaders spoke, it was done in Chinese.

In 2015, I interviewed one of Nigeria's foremost linguists, Kola Tubosun. He told me about his irritation with Nigerian leaders who go to the United Nations and spoke English. My position, then, was that the leaders had no option because English is Nigeria's unifying language. But the linguist politely disagreed, stressing that a Nigerian leader who spoke Hausa or Yoruba at an international summit wasn't dividing the country, but reminding his peers that he has a place in the world beyond the boundaries created by white men. Rather, the use of English, the linguist suggested, was the shackling of Nigerian identity into the shallow frames constructed by British colonialism.

The linguist's words came back to haunt me during my time in China. Previously, I had been unable to imagine a world without English as the measure of intelligence, as a symbol of power. I spoke Yoruba growing up, but it was regarded as a sign of mediocrity in the schools I attended. We filled forms in English. We recited the National Anthem and Pledge in English. We were taught mathematics in English. My entire education was built on the foundation that English is the sole route to knowledge and influence in the world. In a lot of ways, it is. But here I was, in a land where English was second place.

English's power in the world, even in China, is indisputable. Most of the young Chinese people I met could speak and were trying to improve their proficiency. Some even declared open envy for my fluency and asked for tips. But their relationship with Chinese was fundamental to how they saw the world.

★

When I wasn't learning Chinese, I was at Renmin University (Renda), the school where I had been admitted into for a Masters program. It is one of China's most prestigious universities, with an especially strong social sciences pedigree. The school has its roots in the CPC's revolutionary struggle against Japanese aggression and has a number of veritable alumni, including Liu Quangdong, one of China's richest men and founder of JD.com, the e-commerce behemoth.

I still remember my first time. Ensconced on Zhongguancun road, one of the most famous streets in Beijing, Renda showed up unannounced. It wasn't there, and then it was. The driver veered right and went through a modest gate. The wine-coloured buildings and the black and yellow speed-bumps were one of the first things I noticed as the bus rolled through the campus before eventually making a stop in front of the International Students office. I was struck, deeply, by the university's clean and orderly spaces. It felt like a place where knowledge could live, and breed.

Throughout my stay in China, Renda was one of the few places I returned to frequently, alone, for the sole purpose of exploring the spaces. If I had a free day, I'll put my laptop in a bag, ride the subway, find a quiet classroom, and write or do whatever I had earmarked for the day. Then, as the sun moved west, I'd find a bike and tour the grounds, mentally mapping every detail, the gardens, the squares, the library, the residential quarters, the cafeterias. When I shared my fascination with my brother, who was studying at the time in Moscow and had been to the United States, he laughed and said 'then you should go see Harvard'. But Renda was my Harvard. It was the first institution I attended that showed me what a great university could feel like.

As far as the CAPC program was concerned, we had two major businesses at the university. One was related to a series of lectures about Chinese culture, politics and media, delivered by a cast of eminent Chinese scholars and researchers. The other was related to the Masters Program.

The lecture series started brightly, but lost its appeal after a few months, partly because the content started to feel repetitive. Most of the scholars took a bird-eye view approach in their discussions and it was only a matter of time before some people got bored hearing the same details of how, for example, China is a developing country because the western and eastern sections of the country have contrasting development indices. But the series also formed part of the coursework for the Masters program, so I attended virtually every session.

The Masters program was open to only a select few from the African and Asian group. We took six courses during the session, including a Chinese Language course. But it was difficult, since we had to combine our work as journalists, travelling across the country, with being students. The CAPC and Renda team performed a lot of acrobatics to work around our ever-busy schedule, fixing make-up classes and securing ad-hoc spaces at the DRC.

The courses were English-taught and the professors were mostly western-trained with requisite international exposure. Dr. Qin Lin, who had done graduate work at Columbia University, taught us an elective course, Global Journalism and Public Diplomacy. She was a slight woman with sharp, penetrative glances and a simmering intelligence. Her classes were discussion-led, punctuated only by short, pithy comments. Usually, she ended the class with a speech, which I took to be a summary of her thoughts over the course of the almost three-hour long conversation. Dong Chenyu, who taught us Theories of Communication and Journalism, was the raconteur. Chubby and casual, he told a multitude of stories, to explain the theories. He was fascinating. Dr. Shuya Pan was less exciting, but that was mostly due to her course title, Applied Communications Research Methods, which required a certain level of methodical approach and mathematical engagement. In all her classes, she had a smile on her face as she, and we, painstakingly went through perhaps what are the most important lessons for graduate students: how to conduct great research.

Another favourite professor was Dr Sophie Sun Ping, who taught us Contemporary Chinese Politics,

Economy and Culture. She seemed to combine raw intelligence, boundless curiosity and a honest desire to engage and help her students succeed. When one of my friends, back home, asked me to put him in touch with a Chinese professor, it was Dr Sophie I went to and she gladly agreed.

But at the end of our stay in China, we would learn that CAPC fellows will no longer be permitted to participate, concurrently, in the Masters program. We were the first set of fellows that had gotten the scholarship, and we were going to be the last. While we spent a considerable amount of time attending classes, writing papers and making presentations, the academic demands, I suspect, were less rigorous than should be usually required for the average Master's degree. That was due, obviously, to our other pressing responsibilities as journalists, which, on its own, required enormous mental and physical resources to fulfill. Before I left for China, Mr Fan, the Embassy officer who facilitated my trip, had told me those ten months were set to be one of the busiest periods of my life. And I was prepared for that. But not everyone in the class agreed with me, when it appeared I was instigating the professors for more workload, through my capacity as the class representative. I empathised with their position. Sometimes, classes were fixed a day after returning from some remote region and we had to deal with jetlag, after hours on a plane. But I knew, intuitively, that we were not doing enough.

However, the reason given for the scholarship's cancellation was the fact that we were working as reporters, while living in China on a student visa. That, apparently, was a technical error that had been missed in designing the scholarship. Foreigners living in China through a student visa are not expected to work, although in August 2018, the Ministry of Education announced that foreign students could now take part-time jobs, if they got approval from their academic institutions and immigration authorities.

The cancellation cast doubts on our future as Renda students, but the professor coordinating the scholarship, Zhang Di, assured us that our status wasn't threatened by the decision. I believed him. It was easy to see that the situation was beyond him and he was doing what he could. My only comment, when he met us to discuss the issues, was that a more regular flow of communication should be established between the school and us, so as to dispel any budding misconceptions.

Personally, my time at Renda had increased the appeal of academic scholarship, as a career. During my undergraduate years, some of my professors believed

I had the qualities to do more theoretical work. But I was already seduced by the combative, fast-paced nature of journalism. Besides, I never wanted to do more theoretical work in a Nigerian university and I didn't have the money or excellent academic records to pursue graduate studies abroad. So I stuck with journalism, laboring through an avalanche of doubts and, sometimes, despair.

But, at Renda, I realised that it was quite possible to do great work. There was fast Wi-Fi and the school's digital library was subscribed to a variety of exciting journals. I greedily downloaded papers from the library onto my computer, afraid that I could lose access the next minute. And I began to explore a research area I wanted to focus on.

When we were asked whether we wanted to submit a portfolio of our journalism work or write a dissertation as conditions for satisfying the requirements of the Master's degree, I had no hesitation in choosing the latter. I was even ready to take a break off journalism to write it. I asked Prof Zhang if I could stay at the International Students dormitory for another year, to focus on the dissertation. The dormitory was quiet and, even with roommates, quite comfortable - the power didn't go off and there was running water. But the terms of the scholarship, as had been clearly enunciated even before I left Nigeria, was that we would complete the dissertation in our home countries. When it was time to leave China, I bought a lamp and a printer and stored my digital library access details in multiple places. I couldn't let it disappear, under any circumstances.

★

I also learnt how to ride a bicycle in Beijing. From our first days, I wondered why there were lots of bicycles on the sidewalk. Then I learnt, from Hafyza and Billy, that the bikes could be unlocked through mobile apps. But I didn't start learning until summer, when one of the ride-sharing companies, Mobike, scrapped a key part of its business model by dropping the need for deposits in order to ride a bike. The company said the decision was spurred by tests in about 100 markets, which led to a significant boost in users. So during summer, I made my first trip, with Tlotlo and Trix offering me lessons.

And I went on to spend more than 100 RMB on solo trips, travelled more than 145 km, burnt an excess of 15,000 calories, and saved the earth not less than 17.4kg in carbon emissions.

As soon as I mastered the required techniques, I rode everywhere, to the supermarket, to the subway stations, to official meetings. I rode a lot at night too, going for tens of kilometres into unchartered areas with only the map on my phone as a guide. They were some of the most thrilling experiences of my life.

One evening that summer, I commuted on Beijing's Subway Line 2 to rendezvous with a friend on Changchun Street. We were scheduled to meet up and ride across town. While walking towards the meeting spot, I found a sparkling Mobike on the sidewalk and promptly retrieved my cell-phone, opened the Mobike app and pointed my camera towards the QR code lodged in between the bike's two handles. The scanning was successful but the usual *whirling click* of the bike's lock did not occur. On my cell-phone's screen, a pop-up box announced that *this particular trip was* free: in other words, someone had forgotten to lock up the bike after use. I pushed back the bike-stand and hopped on it, cycling away, the sound of whistling in my head.

My friend was late. So I cycled some more along the sidewalk, which was shaded by trees and shadows of pedestrians hustling by. Then my phone beeped. She had arrived, but I had to cross the road. So I turned the bike around and cycled back and waited at the traffic light. And it was there she emerged from the group of people on the sidewalk, her face decorated with smiles, like graffiti.

Then we set out to look for the second Mobike, continuing on the sidewalk, she with a small bag strapped to her back. I was off the bike, steering it by hand.

Every bike-sharing app, whether it is Mobike or Ofo or Hellobike, has a mapping feature that lets you look into your cell-phone and see if there are available bikes near you. On the route we had chosen to follow that evening, we spotted several orange dots. So, confidence was high. The second one we found clicked open but there was a problem with the chain.

So we walked on, discussing, with one eye on the next Mobike. We would see the glow of orange on a bike far ahead and we would scream, relieved that we had finally struck gold, only to realise that it was a private bike or some other bike-sharing company. We passed a lot of Ofos, but both of us didn't have a subscription. Once, we crossed the blue glow of a subway station and found a couple of Mobikes littered on the sidewalk. But each one was damaged: broken spokes, a handle sawed off, an inexistent chain.

At that point, we had walked for more than two miles, way past the duration of the average Mobike trip, which lasts for <u>about 1.8 miles</u>. Our legs were tired, more from anxiety than physical stress. We flirted with ending the night with a subway ride or hail a Didi. But the conversation was good and we kept walking. After we crossed the umpteenth intersection however, my friend turned to me and asked, "Where are all the fucking Mobikes?"

I reasoned that since it was already several minutes to midnight, most people were holed up somewhere, stationary, waiting for the next sunrise. The problem then, I suggested to my friend, was that we had been walking on major roads. Instead, we had to use the feeder roads and navigate into residential streets. My conclusion was based on two assumptions. The first one was that it was summer and most people, especially those who use the subway, would rather cycle home than walk even if the distance was short. The second one, borrowing heavily from the first, was that if people were cycling home, no one was cycling back at midnight.

We veered off the main roads and soon found ourselves in the middle of a hutong, wandering between closed shops and small structures that huddled together like vertical stack of cards. And, indeed, the Mobikes started to appear, like a revelation, in front of people's homes. There was so much to choose from, like a glut.

Later, my friend told me about how people in the apartment building she lived would pick up Mobikes and ride them into their apartment so they wouldn't have to look for one in the morning. I was surprised but anti-social behaviour related to the bike-sharing industry is quite common. Two weeks after Mobike introduced some 1,000 shiny new bikes to Manchester, UK, people reported spotting the bikes in the canal, in bins and stashed in people's gardens. Some of the bike's GPS trackers had even been disabled and the wheel locks at the back smashed off. Just a little over a year after it was launched in the city, Mobike had to pull out of Manchester, citing the loss of 10% of its bikes each month to theft and vandalism.

To combat anti-social behaviour, Mobike has a credit score system that allocates points to users for good behaviour and dock points for bad behaviour. In February 2018, the company made a global update to the system, splitting it into five categories: 0-300 is Poor, 301-500 is Fair, 501-600 is Good, 601-700 is Excellent and 701-1000 is Outstanding. The scores are reappraised on a monthly basis.

My scores were just above average.

SHANGHAI

i clocked 24 in July and spent the entire day
indoors, replying to congratulatory messages.
Ahlem, God bless her soul, baked me the sweetest
chocolate cake ever and Tlotlo brought some candles.
Trix and Omphi dropped by and shared in the cake
and I played some music. It was a quiet, satisfying
day.

On July 16, we boarded a flight to Shanghai
Hongqiao Airport. On arrival, we visited the
Shanghai Urban History Exhibition Hall and the
Shanghai Oriental Pearl Tower, which was once the
tallest structure in China. Both sites swarmed with
tourists. We had dinner at the Revolving Restaurant
inside the Pearl Tower, which has an exhilarating
view of the Bund.

The next day, we visited the historical site of the
first CPC conference. In October 2017, Xi Jinping,
along with six other Politburo Standing Committee
members, had paid a visit to the same place, a

spartan, grey brick building on Xingye Road. "The Communist Party was born here," Xi had said, "these are the roots of the party."

Apart from hosting the site of the First National Congress of the CPC, it is also home to the site of the Second National Congress located on Chengdu Road and former residences of venerable, past Chinese leaders, Dr. Sun Yat-Sen, Mao Zedong and Zhou Enlai.

Some of the city's other cultural historic sites include the well-preserved Yuyuan Garden which was constructed in 1559, the Longhua Temple in Xuhui District, a Buddhist temple that was built in 247 AD, the Confucius Temple that was built in 1219, the Square Pagoda in Songjiang District that was built in 949, and many more.

Shanghai's cultural history is an integral part of what makes the city attractive to those who flock in; city authorities know this and have moved to ramp up tourism infrastructure, constructing impressive facilities such as the Oriental Tower, a 468-meter tall edifice. At 263 meters, tourists can get a bird's eye-view of the city and at 267 meters high sits the rotating restaurant, where we had dinner on the first day. At the ground floor of the structure is a historical museum featuring the city's history, including life-like representations of old Shanghai streets. The museum's realism is so heavy that, upon visiting, it was hard to stay rooted in the 21st century.

In 2017, the added value of the city's tourism sector reached 188.824 billion RMB. With a brand of economic planning that focuses on improving infrastructure, that number can only go in one direction: upward.

After leaving Xingye Road, we met with leaders of the Shanghai Municipal Foreign Affairs Office, including the Deputy Director-General, Mr Fu Jihong, who talked about the Shanghai dream, one which imagines a city that is the most desirable, not just in China, but in the world. "We have to be enterprising and committed," Mr Jihong said, "we have to be persistent."

Shanghai is becoming one of the world's most sophisticated cities. In 2017, its per capita GDP was $18,450. It is home to a total of 625 multinational companies and 426 foreign-funded Research and Development (R&D) centres, and also an important shipping centre, operating some of the busiest ports in the world.

There are theories, of course, to why Shanghai has flourished. There are those who attribute its success to its unique location, on the estuary of the Yangtze River, facing the Pacific. There are also theories that point to its relatively early contact with foreign merchants. A much rounded and less circumstantial response will have to be China's economic revival. According to data from city authorities, in 1978, the city's fiscal revenue was 16.922 billion RMB; in 2017, it had increased by 3,825 per cent at 664.226 billion RMB.

Meanwhile, these numbers have had real world effects. In Shanghai, life expectancy is now 83, as good as Switzerland.

Our second morning in Shanghai was spent touring Zhangjiang Hi-Tech Park, in the city's northern district of Pudong. Described by some as China's Silicon Valley, the park is a reflection of China's ambition to transform Shanghai into a high-tech development zone capable of global leadership.

In 2017, the park announced expansion plans to rebrand itself as a 'Science City'. Already home to more than 600 hundred companies and employing over 350,000 people, the park will be expanded to some 94 square kilometres with new infrastructure, such as new housing units, scheduled to be constructed.

On what sort of innovative work had been done at the park since it was founded in 1992, Deputy Director-General of the Zhangjiang Administration Bureau, Jun Wu, touted ground-breaking research in several fields, especially in biomedicine. Just before we visited, a Chinese research group with roots in the park had announced progress in developing a drug, GV-971, which can be used to treat Alzheimer's disease after a 21-year study.

Zhangjiang's success is rooted in its ability to help companies scale faster. Microport, a company that describes its goal as "improving human life through the practical application of innovative science", set up shop as a small outfit in Zhangjiang in 1998. 20 years later, the company has grown to become a premier medical solution provider covering 10 major medical disciplines including interventional cardiology, orthopedics, cardiac rhythm management, electrophysiology, interventional radiology, diabetes and endocrine management, surgical management, and others. It has over 260 products currently approved for use in over 5,000 hospitals worldwide and its products are used on patients every 12 seconds, according to company data.

"We probably would not have grown so fast if we had set up shop somewhere else," a spokeswoman for the company, Bonnie Xia, told me while we toured its product showrooms. "We received a lot of support from the trade leagues and the Zhangjiang Investment Company which helped us to attract talent and investors."

But Wu, the Zhangjiang technocrat, believes

the park's administrators need to do more if Shanghai is to become a world-class, hi-tech city. He admitted that attracting talent remains a thorny problem, while there is need for the park to record more technological breakthroughs. "We also aim to improve cooperation between China and other foreign states," he said. He was, however, optimistic of a bright future. There is a documented plan to transform Shanghai into a high-tech development city by 2035, but Wu believes that by 2020, when most of the new planned infrastructure projects in Zhangjiang would have been completed, the dream would be palpable. "Come after the year 2020," he said, "you will experience a huge transformation."

Later that evening, we rode on the Shanghai Metro, which is reputed to be the world's largest rapid transit system by route length. It felt similar to Beijing's, but it was also more modern and trafficked.

Our fourth day was spent at Binjiang Park, which afforded us a good view of the Huangpu River and the Bund. Then, when dusk came, we boarded a ferry to get a feel of the River itself. I took lots of pictures.

On the fifth day, we travelled to Chongming Island, a beautiful getaway resort just one hour drive from Central Shanghai. There, a Counsellor at the Information Department of the Chinese Ministry of Foreign Affairs, Mr Liu Yutong, said: "I believe

Shanghai will become an international Metropolitan centre. This is completely irreversible."

Our translator for the Shanghai trip was Linda Wang, an agile lady with attractive, sharp features who spoke English without an accent. Wang was born in Dalian, a modern, port city in China's Liaoning Province. If the map of China is a chicken, Dalian is right at the jaw. It was occupied by the Russians in 1898 and has streets lined with Russian-styled architecture.

A precocious student, Wang had flair for languages and she met great professional interpreters who encouraged her to work in the field. After High School in Dalian, she left for Sydney, Australia for University education. When she returned home and was looking to improve her skills, she moved to Shanghai and enrolled at the Shanghai International Studies University for Interpreting and Translation.

"Growing up, skyscrapers and modern facilities were not alien to me," Wang said. But Shanghai was something different. It was our last evening in Shanghai and we were sitting in the lobby of our residence hotel.

"The cool thing about working as an interpreter is that you get to see lots of different things and interact with government officials," she said. "Dalian is a very modern city too, but one thing about Shanghai is that it is very efficient. The government officials mean what they say and I think they are passionate about what they do. When you speak with them, you can feel that they are genuinely proud of what they do. I don't see that everywhere. Everyone loves where they come from, but Shanghai people are especially proud of Shanghai. Once, I was talking to a bus driver and asking him about the traffic peak time and how it wasn't so bad, since we were not stuck, his response was that, 'yes, that's because we have very good management'."

In Wang's telling, Shanghai is a city that you have a love-hate relationship with. You hate it because it is very fast and realistic, which comes with a lot of pressure, but you love it because the transportation is very convenient, the security excellent (you can walk at 2am without any fear) and there is a staggering amount of public amenities to take advantage of. "A lot of people I know want to stay here, buy a house, get married and have children," she said. "I am happy here. If you stay here for too long, there is no way you can go to another city. Once, I visited Shenzhen and Guangzhou – these are very developed cities – but I stayed there and was missing Shanghai."

THE PEOPLE'S MEDIA

*M*y brother arrived Beijing in August. He flew in from Moscow where he had just completed a Masters degree in Public Policy. In the taxi to the DRC, he spoke glowingly about the grandness of the Russian capital, the parliament buildings and the subway, and lectured me on the fine details of state-directed economies. Of course, we also talked about the increasing fragility at home.

After about six months of living in China, it felt refreshing to see him. It was the first time we were meeting since he left for eastern Europe in 2016. I bought him a lot of McDonalds as he tried to adjust to the time-zone and also made him soup and rice. But he soon took over the kitchen. When he flew to Nigeria two weeks later, he left multiple bowls of soup for me in the refrigerator.

I took him out to a Brazilian show in Beijing and he wandered, alone, to Tiananmen square. Together, we took a trip to the Great Wall. We used the Subway, then took the bus and bought strange street food to the delight of several Chinese tourists, who couldn't get enough of the two jolly black men with funny hair.

But, during his two weeks stay in Beijing, we didn't spend a lot of time together, because August was also when I had my internship at Xinhuanet.com, the digital arm of China's Xinhua News Agency.

At this point, we had visited several media houses in Beijing and across China, admiring the state-of-the-art equipment and paying attention to their modus operandi. The Chinese don't believe the media should be independent; instead, it should serve as an extension of government communication efforts, in this case the CPC's agenda. The thinking is that since the CPC exists for the good of the people, by toeing the party line, the media was definitely serving the people. For me, the internship was an opportunity to experience, first hand, how Chinese journalists operate within the CPC bubble. Some of my colleagues were posted to CGTN, Global Times, CRI. Hazem, the Egyptian, joined me at Xinhuanet.

The first thing I remember about Xinhuanet is Sherry, the editor who attended to us on our first day of resumption. She sounded nervous as she addressed our group, which included journalists from Latin America and Southeast Asia, about the need to sign a document, certifying our internship status. But it was written in Chinese and the group demanded for it to be translated into English. After asking her a few questions, I signed the document, but the others baulked, which got her frustrated.

Hazem later told me I shouldn't have signed. But I didn't see the point. We had come for a one-month internship and the document, as she had explained, had been designed for Chinese interns. However, I didn't fault their decision not to sign. They were apprehensive about clauses that could create conflict with their media houses back home. Since I didn't have a binding contract back home, I didn't have those worries.

I met a lot of wonderful people at Xinhuanet's newsroom. Renata was a Brazilian working in the Portuguese section, but her English was great. She had a kind smile and a scooter. I rode with her several times. Once, we rode to a park, where she told me how she had made the move to China and her dreams to become an academic. And she was in love with Davido.

There wasn't so much to do in the newsroom. I usually arrived early and sat at the designated desk, writing my own stories. Then, when the music for the daily stretch exercises came on, I joined in, mimicking my Chinese colleagues; They always looked amused that I took part. Behind me was Veronica, who was also in the Portuguese section. She didn't speak any English, but we got along pretty well. Carol, an intern in the French section, usually sauntered over to my desk to talk. She was a party member and was engaged in several activities promoting Chinese culture. When she ended her internship, one week before mine ended, she gifted me a miniature sculpture of a Chinese scholar. It was one of the best presents I received in China.

My first official assignment for the website was to interview Zeng Aiping, the Deputy Executive Director of the China-Asean African Cooperation Centre. He was a humorous man who spoke with a diplomat's calm. When I asked him why China doesn't focus on human rights in Africa, he told me economic development is the best guarantee of human rights. Our approach to Africa is more practical, more concrete, more tangible," he said. "We help African countries build infrastructure. This is tangible. Everybody can see this and feel it."

My next assignment was with Caroline, an adorable, if edgy, lady who made numerous wide-eyed expressions. She had just returned from the UK, where she had gone for graduate studies. We were to go to Renda and cover a Think Tank forum. But she was nervous, because it was the first time she would be going 'alone' to the field. I assured her everything was going to be fine. Although most of the forum was conducted in Chinese, I collected the forum's papers and interviewed panelists on the sidelines. Then I wrote and sent her two news stories, which she was to translate into Chinese. She was grateful. Few days before I left China, she hosted me to a hot pot meal in Sanlitun.

On most days, I ate at the cafeteria, which was usually crowded. Ashley, a bespectacled lady in the English department, was a big help. She paid with her card while we refunded her via Wechat, before we got our own cards. And she told me about the big English novels she was reading. She, too, had travelled abroad, to the United States.

Virtually everyone in the newsroom had been a foreigner once, so I guess they knew what it was like to be different, to be a minority. I never felt uncomfortable during my time there. It was an opportunity to experience how a Chinese newsroom worked. I found it boring, of course, because no one was shouting across the hall or debating a comment or screaming 'breaking news'. It felt regimented and iron-clad and monotonous. But I had great conversations with the people I met there.

★

In the middle of the internship, Sherry asked me if I would like to travel to a city in Southwest China, Bijie. It was a trip to learn more about China's poverty alleviation efforts. I told her I would go.

Bijie is a prefecture-level city in China's northwestern Guizhou Province with a sub-tropical climate. To get there, we boarded a three-hour flight from Beijing to Guiyang Longdongbao airport and then took a three-hour bus ride through roads flanked by rolling mountains, lush vegetation, stunning valleys. The road passed through several tunnels.

At Dafang County, one of six counties in Bijie, we visited a pure Angus breeding farm. The clouds were sour, pregnant with imminent rainfall. At the bottom edge of a sloping field, cows grazed as Chinese officials addressed the group.

To combat poverty in Dafang County, the Chinese government partnered with the private sector (in this case: Evergrande Group) to import Angus cattle from Australia and set up a breeding farm.

"We brought an industry into China so that it can enrich farmers and improve their income," Vice president of Evergrande, Long Baozheng, said.

The government is mainly responsible for policy

support and logistics services, while Evergrande is responsible for the construction of the breeding farm and providing the start-up cows.

The partnership also involves a leading beef cattle production company in China, China Hengrui, which is responsible for professional farming, processing and sales.

"We believe this is the fastest way to increase the poor farmer's income," Mr Long said. "We do not change their lifestyle. They still plant their maize, which is their original source of income. But now they can supplement their income and increase it by more than a hundred per cent."

The breeding farm covers an area of 173.6 acres with a total investment of 13 million RMB. The number of designed breeding stocks is 1,000, which was completed and put into use in June 2016.

Now, according to Mr Long, the enterprise in Dafang County now boasts of about 30,000 cows. The target for next year is 50,000. "We want to be able to raise 150,000 in the future," he said.

This initiative has seen the local farmers' income rise to as high as 30,000 RMB per year. And each household receives dividends from profit derived from the cattle business.

Also, the presence of the breeding farm has driven the development of silage planting, processing and transportation in Dafang County.

At Hengda Village, which is in Fenda Town of Dafang County, the pregnant clouds convulsed and burst, filling the earth with fat, innumerable drops of water. The group scampered towards shelter.

We were visiting one of the first resettlement sites of Evergrande Group Poverty Alleviation Project in Dafang County and just ahead were rows of double-storied buildings. The porches provided shelter. Then, at one of the buildings, as the rain hammered down, the door swung open and a curious head poked out.

Zhong Zhenying was apparently not expecting visitors. But the rain and people on her doorstep must have drawn her attention. She invited us into her home. Inside, it was warm

Zhenying, who is 83, was a poverty alleviation beneficiary in Dafang. She showed us pictures of her old home, a hut-styled building surrounded by shrubbery, which she had shared with her husband, son and grandson. But, one year ago, she moved to her new home constructed by Evergrande. "We are very happy here," she said.

Hengda Village, like most poverty alleviation schemes in China, is also a public-private sector initiative. The government is responsible for land acquisition and demolition, and access to basic amenities such as water, electricity, and roads. But

Evergrande takes care of the housing construction and the purchase of necessary household items such as furniture and electrical appliances.

The total investment of the project is 10 million RMB and the village covers an area of 21.67 acres with a building area of 3560 meters. It can accommodate 42 households. Till date, more than 30 households have moved in.

Also, in order to ensure stable income for the relocated households, Evergrande Group built 443 standardized vegetable greenhouses around the village. Each household is entitled to two greenhouses. Income within the community has risen as high as 20,000 RMB per year.

Shandong Sanyuanzhu Group was then invited to carry out the unified management of the greenhouses. At the end of the year, the group pays dividends to the local households.

At an elevated platform that overlooked a vast stretch of kiwifruit plantation in Haizi Village somewhere in Bijie, Chen Zhigang, the Deputy Director of the State Council Poverty Alleviation Office, shared some tips about why poverty alleviation had succeeded in Bijie. A passionate man with words, he noted that civil societies had been utilised to ensure that the people took responsibility for the development of their villages.

To combat poverty, he opined, it was not enough to give handouts to poor people. Instead, they should be empowered through employment. "That's why you need to create industries in the rural areas and make the people self-reliant," he said. "Haizi is a typical agriculture Village. But when we renovated their house, we also introduced agriculture products like the kiwi fruit which increases their income by ten times than when they just plant maize."

This sort of creativity, in the long run, also leads to agricultural tourism, which will also help the people increase their income step by step, he said.

Responding to a question on how difficult it had been to convince the people to adopt new practices and revamp their villages, Mr Zhigang stressed that it was important to mobilise the people, to preach to them to help themselves to become self-reliant. "You need to educate them that they can change their own fate," he said, "and our experience is that we use the way that people do things to help them do things."

He explained that when the house renovations started, not every household was willing to cooperate. But after some model houses had been built and the result was there for all to see, the others stepped in.

"We also show them blueprints of what the future can be if they work hard," he said. "We facilitate tours to other successful villages. In that way, they realise that good things don't just fall from the sky. You have to work hard to get it. So it happens that people want to compete with each other. Villages want to compete with each other. This is human nature and we use it to promote development."

★

When I returned to Beijing, my brother was already packing his bags, to return to Nigeria. On the day he was to leave, I took him to a massage parlour. Caroline helped us find it. I saw him off at the airport and returned to an empty apartment. But, the next day, I was back at Xinhuanet, moving through the motions, counting down to the most important summit of the year: the Forum on China and Africa Cooperation (FOCAC).

THE BIG SUMMIT

*t*he FOCAC summit, in September, was the official highlight of our stay in China. Virtually every African president was expected in Beijing. We started our press accreditation several months earlier. And the closer it got, the greater the anticipation. The skies in Beijing became clearer and I polished my notes, in preparation for a major reporting assignment.

There were a number of pre-forum conferences and we attended most of them, including media, think tank and ministerial forums. Journalists, scholars and government officials from across Africa and China flew into Beijing for these meetings. The city buzzed. At the ministerial summit, which held at the cusp of the FOCAC summit, I spoke to two Nigerian federal ministers, Udo Udoma and Geoffrey Onyeama, and they told me Nigerian presence in China was geared towards securing more infrastructure loans from China. President Muhammadu Buhari led the Nigerian delegation, which included a cast of assorted State Governors.

FOCAC is the highest policy-shaping tool for Africa-China relations. The decisions taken at the meeting is the blueprint through which China engages with African countries over a period of years. Although the first forum was held in 2006, in Beijing, top African and Chinese ministers had been meeting under the China-Africa Consultative Forum (CACF) since 2000. The second FOCAC forum was held in South Africa, in 2015. The next summit, in 2021, is scheduled to hold in Dakar, Senegal.

I attended several Chinese state reception of African leaders, including South Africa's Cyril Ramaphosa. For these visits, we arrived at the Great Hall hours before the leaders appeared and went through thorough security checks. Then we had to proceed to an elevated stand where cameras could be positioned. The waiting period provided opportunities to talk to Chinese journalists covering the event. Everyone stopped twittering to pay attention when the leaders appeared with their respective delegates. The short procession were spiced up by school children waving and singing and a military brigade marching and saluting.

After the public reception, we would be ushered into a room where the school children have their rehearsals. The rooms in the Great Hall are commodious and airy and heavily rugged.

It takes a while, but we would get called to witness the signing of MoUs between African and Chinese leaders. The Africans sat on one side of the long table, while the Chinese sat on the other. The mood was usually cheery and relaxed.

Some of my colleagues, whose leaders we observed at the Great Hall, complained of not being able to get access to details of the MoUs that were being signed. I had similar worries, as I tracked the reporting of President Buhari's activities in China. On the day he left Nigeria, a press release was disseminated announcing that the President was to sign off on a $328 million provided by the Export-Import Bank of China to grow Nigeria's Information and Communication Technology sector. Also, Buhari was to witness the signing of the Belt and Road Initiative MoU and no fewer than 25 other MoUs that cut across various government parastatals.

On September 3, President Xi Jinping gave a speech at the Great Hall and announced a $60 billion financial package for Africa. The $60 billion included $15 billion in grants, interest-free loans and concessional loans, $20 billion in credit lines and a $10 billion special fund for development financing. The remaining $10 billion would be invested by

Chinese companies in Africa over the next three years.

The announcement set off a diverse range of views both online and offline. The Chinese interpreted it as a sign of China's magnanimity and critics, mostly from the West, said it was another sign that China was intent on burdening Africa with debt. A number of foreign correspondents called me, asking for my views. But I didn't have one. I felt it was racist to assume that all the African leaders present at the summit didn't understand the gravity of the deals they were signing on, but Africa also has serious governance issues that makes mockery of the best intentions.

At the FOCAC Press Centre, which was equipped with desktop computers connected to an unrestricted internet, several Chinese reporters also asked for my views on China's relationship with Africa. It's great, I would say, and then go on to talk about the number one problem I thought was plaguing the relationship: transparency. China needs to be more transparent was probably my favorite phrase. Most of the reporters didn't flinch at the criticism, but some weren't so tolerant. You are too critical, one woman said and stomped out of the room. It was an amusing scene. Apparently, she couldn't believe an African could have anything 'bad' to say about China after their President had just announced a $60 billion 'gift' for the continent.

For the summit's closing press conference, we headed to the Great Hall again, where we waited for almost six hours before President Xi appeared with Mr Ramaphosa and Senegalese President Macky Sall, who became the new African FOCAC co-chair. They announced the adoption of two documents: the "Beijing Declaration - Toward an Even Stronger China-Africa Community with a Shared Future" and the "FOCAC Beijing Action Plan (2019 - 2021)". The documents underlined China's commitment to maintaining its sunny relationship with African countries.

I didn't learn a lot of new things attending the summit. Everything went according to plan. But I did go away with the conviction that if Africa was to benefit from the plans hatched in Beijing, a lot will depend on the quality of leadership back home.

LAST DAYS

*a*fter the September summit, things began to peter out. We still had to travel to more provinces but the sense of finality hovered. Home was calling.

In October, we travelled, first, to Jincheng, a city about 700km southwest of Beijing. We took a flight to Luoyang city, then travelled by bus to Jincheng. At the airport, the city officials were friendly and handed us bottles of water. The road into the city traversed through a series of hills and coal mines and vast stretches of vegetation.

Jincheng is not a big city, but it has a lot of history. Some say it is a cradle of Chinese civilisation, an area that was settled by man 20,000 years ago. There are stories of Confucius passing through and major wars like the Battle of Changping being associated with its history. The city has huge reserves of coal bed methane, dolomite, limestone and bauxite, making it an important economic zone for the Chinese government.

After checking into the hotel, we visited Huangcheng village, where we toured the Royal Prime Minister's Palace. The locals, mostly seniors, crowded out in front of their homes, staring curiously at our group. Foreigners, their eyes seemed to say, where have they come from?

The village has a lot of centuries-old *Siheyuan* structures. A *Siheyuan* is a courtyard surrounded by buildings on all four sides. I had seen similar structures in Beijing. Here, they had been properly preserved too, as far as I could tell. The streets were clean and narrow (more like alleys).

The Prime Minister's Palace, built by a famous prime minister of the Qing Dynasty, Chen Tingjing, covers a sightseeing area of thousands of square meters. There are eight large courtyards in the inner city, especially the particularly noticeable 30m high seven-storey Heshan Tower in which there are wells, stone roller, grinder and a secret channel to go out of the city.

As the sun went down, we drove to Zhongzhuang village, less than five minutes away, for a 'special dinner' - the Eight to Eight feast. I sat at a table with one of the local officials, an amiable woman named Kathy. She told us that this was a special feast reserved for royalty. It consisted of a variety of soups and vegetables dishes.

After the meal, we attended a night-time cultural streetshow in Guoyu. A crowd gathered around the performers, who beat drums and danced in flamboyant red costumes. Parents put their kids on their neck, so they could have a good view. Then we went back to our hotel, weary.

The next day, we travelled by bus to Gaoping to visit the Tombs of Yandi mausoleum. Emperor Yandi is reputed to be the first ancestor of the Chinese nation and the god of agriculture. Then we visited the Jilier Lu Silk cultural park, also in Gaoping, where we saw a display of high quality, value-added silk products like curtains and bedsheets. Some of the items cost as much as 60,000 RMB.

After Jilier Lu and lunch, we went to Jintian Agriculture in Gaoping. We were served fresh greens and given a tour of the farm before leaving for Situ Town, where we walked through an alley of restaurants. I bought a soup of meatballs (it tasted like beef) and shared with others. After dinner, we witnessed another cultural performance. This time not a street-show. We sat in an open-roof theatre. On the stage, a mercurial display of fire and drums mesmerised us for almost an hour. I couldn't grasp the narrative, but it was a fascinating work of art.

The next day we visited two water treatment projects. Jincheng, as I mentioned earlier, is a coal city. And, although a boon for power, coal is dirty. So I think the officials wanted us to see that the government understood and was paying attention to the environment. We also had time to visit the city's industrial park, which is primed to attract investors. Jincheng is already famous for its strength in smelting and casting, so the government wants to build on that and develop the city into a high and medium-end manufacturing centre. They have a number of plans in place, including offering academics up to 12 million RMB to settle there and conduct research.

We went back to Beijing later that day.

Kathy texted me on Wechat several weeks after. I had promised to file a report about Jincheng to my newspaper back home. And she wanted to see it. But I never filed the report. I had tried to, but just couldn't figure out the structure. I told her I was going to let her know when I did, and she sent me happiness emojis. "So expect," she wrote.

★

In October, we also went to Yangzhou in Jiangsu province, to attend the World Canal Cities Forum. After the Forum, which lasted for a day, we toured the famous Shouxi Lake and returned to Beijing the next day. A few days later, we were on our way, again, to Sichuan province, about 2,000km south-west of Beijing.

Our first stop in Sichuan was Yibin, a city with a population of more than 4.5 million people and home to one of China's most famous and luxurious liquor brand, Wuliangye. The brand is so popular that local authorities have named a newly built airport, the Yibin Wuliangye Airport, after it.

We visited the company's 13,000 cellar liquor factory, which is one of the world's largest aromatic liquor-producing facilities and they served us fresh sips of Wuliangye essence, straight from the source. Later, during dinner with company officials, more wine was served and I succeeded in toasting everyone in the room without wobbling, earning me the unofficial designation of a Wuliangye Ambassador. My colleagues talked about it, my alcohol tolerance, for days, even after we left Sichuan.

From Yibin, we travelled by bus to Sichuan's capital city, Chengdu. The city is most famous for two things: pandas and its spicy hotpot. We visited China Lane, a street composed of three parallel alleys (Wide Alley, Narrow Alley and Well Alley). It is a cultural hotspot, where a stranger can go to and grasp the essence of the city's heartbeat in all its rawness, undiluted. The cobbled, narrow alleys are hemmed in by shops displaying colourful souvenir, teahouses, bars, bookshops, high-end restaurants, and an avalanche of stands hawking street food. There are also several services such as ear-cleaning and entertainment facilities like opera and theatre houses.

The lane, which is also known as Jinli Street or Kuanzhai Lane, has existed for hundred of years, when it emerged as a trading centre. In 2008, it re-emerged with a new identity after undergoing heavy renovations and restorations and was opened to the public.

I spoke to several tourists on the streets, most of whom were Chinese. Liu Yizhen, a sombre man in his late twenties had come from Jinlu province in north-east China, with his wife. "I want to explore Chinese history," he told me. "We are here to have a taste of the culture and of the food." Xu Xiansong, a middle-aged Tibetan entrepreneur who had travelled from Anhui province, said it was the promise of Chengdu street-food that lured him to the street. "Then I will like to go to a bar," he said, with a modicum of boyish enthusiasm. "The culture is important, there is a special feeling that people get when they come here," Chen Jin, a local government official added.

The next day, we visited the Qingbaijiang Chengdu International Rail Port, which links China to Europe. The Port is also a free trade zone and is the only one of its kind that solely "relies on the running of the railway," one of the officials said during the briefing; cost of shipping via the railway is reportedly one-eight of sea transportation. Later, I spoke to the Sales Director of beef company, Chengdu Haiyunda, Wang Qi. Since 2013, the company has imported frozen beef from South America and Europe. Then, in 2018, they started importing beef via the rail, from Belarus. "We were very amazed by the cooperation with the express," Mr Wang said. "It only took half a month and the clearance was superfast. And we were able to sell the goods very fast. In the past we wanted quality beef but we didn't have the conditions. It used to take too long. Now it is better."

I have reprinted Mr Wang's quote here, of course, to give you an example of what China wants to achieve with its Belt and Road Initiative: to improve the efficiency of the global flow of goods and services.

On our last day in the city, we went to see the Pandas at the Chengdu Research Base of Giant Panda Breeding; more than four million people go there every year. One of the guides told us that during the Second World War, the sight of a panda eating bamboo was one of the best ways to relieve stress. I think that's still true.

LEAVING, AGAIN

*t*here are many things I haven't told you, Elizabeth. But it is my hope that I have succeeded in offering you a glimpse of what I did in China for ten months. It was an amazing experience living in one of the world's most vibrant cities without worrying about the next paycheck, immersed in the radiant warmth of Chinese culture, the food, the language, the people.

But nothing is free. I paid, in part, with my silence, eyes closed, content with darkness.

Have you heard of Xinjiang? Of the re-education camps? Of people being locked up not for what they've done, but what they could do? And then being transformed through rote. Have you heard?

When someone asked me why I didn't report about Xinjiang while in China, I said I wasn't in China to report on Xinjiang. I was in China to understand Chinese politics and society and how to improve Sino-African relations. It wasn't a lie. That was actually the official responsibility entrusted on me by the Chinese embassy in Abuja. But it wasn't the real reason, because no one limited the things I could write about. I didn't write about it because I was afraid. This fear, like my initial nightmares, didn't come consciously. It just crept up on me, unannounced, like a shadow. I woke up one morning and found it in front of a blank computer screen.

A writer's greatest agony, perhaps, is his inability to write about the things he cares about, the shackling of his vision by the elemental forces of this world, by his poverty, by disease. And this agony, its lingering weight, was a burden that stayed with me throughout my stay.

I cared about Xinjiang, about marxist university student leaders being locked up, because every writer should care about oppression, about injustice. Governments across the world, whether in China or the United States, are wont to place safety over justice, stability over fairness; it is the writer's responsibility to remind people that there can never be lasting peace without equity.

There are apt justifications for this sort of failure - for one, I was a freelancer without a safety net - but excuses don't change the world.

★

I worried, also, about the subliminal effects of China's play in Africa. Trade between China and the continent reached $204.2 billion in 2018; as at the end of 2018, more than 3,700 Chinese companies now do business in Africa, investing over $46 billion, according to data from the Chinese Ministry of Commerce; China is now the second most popular destination for African students studying abroad, surpassing the United States and the United Kingdom. So it should be obvious to you already that Africa-China relations is here to stay. The question that bothers me, however, is how will China, ultimately, shape the continent's future?

Africa, in the words of veteran journalist Howard French, remains "a continent for the taking". Dehumanised by the slave trade, cut to size by western colonialism, and ravaged by the vicious divisiveness of ethnic politics and public corruption, most of us remain tethered to others for our identities, for the construction of our realities and futures. This character, this culture of dependence is why China's role in Africa is important, because it has the opportunity, like the West before it, to leave a mark.

History teaches us to be wary. States are never benevolent by nature. Chinese diplomats like to cite the example of Admiral Zheng He, a Chinese naval commander who sailed across the Indian Ocean, to Africa, in the 15th century, but took no colonies like the Europeans who came after. Zheng is held as a symbol of China's longstanding commitment to noninterference in other people's matters and the Chinese spirit of peace, diplomacy and equality of states. But Zheng He wasn't a connoisseur of harmony. He travelled in an armada and did invade states along his route which did not accept the apparent 'implicit truth' of Chinese superiority. "The modern idea of Zheng He as an explorer is largely a creation of Western scholarship," Howard French writes in *Everything Under the Heavens*. "Zheng He's fleet was actually an armada, in the sense that it carried a powerful army that could be disembarked, and its purpose was to awe the rulers of Southeast Asia and the Indian Ocean into sending tribute to China." In 1411, on his third voyage, Zheng's forces successfully invaded Sri Lanka (Ceylon), for failing to bow before China's hegemony in the region.

But China is not Europe, which has hugely contributed to the underdevelopment of Africa. It is important to make this distinction, even if modern China is currently in the middle of a materialism orgy and will be sorely tempted to also grab what it can, while it still can. Traditional Chinese modesty, steeped in Confucianism, is in contrast to Europe's abrasiveness and warlike, zero-sum conception of the world.

However, to rely on China's rhetoric of a win-win world, built on the ideals of Confucianism, as proof that Africa-China relations will be fair and benefit both sides is a foolish idea. Perhaps the question isn't even how China will act, since we know what China wants already. The important question, really, is how will Africa show up? How is Africa showing up?

It might interest you to know that very few people are interested in answering this question. Some people are still stuck on the 'Is China good for Africa' pseudo-dilemma. Of course China is good for Africa. China has capacity that is useful for Africa's economic development and the continent is strategic to Beijing's vision of a new world order with China at the centre. Anyone who tells you otherwise is wasting your time. China had Japan and the west. Europe had America. Progress doesn't happen in isolation.

Getting past that distracting question helps us to focus on the real one, the one which puts Africa in charge of its own destiny, in the right frame of mind to straighten out the wrinkles in its relationship with China.

Admittedly, the problems in Africa-China relations are numerous, from corruption to trade imbalance to immigration to cultural dissonances. But while there are no quick, easy answers to any of them, they are not impossible to solve.

★

Few weeks to the end of the fellowship, I stumbled across an article shared by American journalist, Eric Fish, on Twitter. It had the headline: 'China is buying good press across the world, one paid journalist at a time.' I hurriedly scanned through the article. It was a profile of the CAPC fellowship which, as described by the reporter, was designed to amplify Chinese propaganda. "I am part of the program," I commented under Fish's post. "Most of the facts in this article are inaccurate. No one tells you to write positive stories or limits what you can do during your stay."

After hours of replying to counter-comments, a reporter from the New York Times sent me a Direct Message. She wanted to chat about the fellowship. We met in Sanlitun one cold afternoon, inside the Bookworm cafe. Essentially, she wanted to know how being in China had changed my worldview. I told her I still believe in democracy, in press freedom. It would take more than ten months of 'luxury' living to change that. I don't think she believed me.

Another Times reporter, who should have joined us for the initial chat, requested for another chance to talk. We met at the lobby of the Renmin Business School building. He was a handsome, Hispanic man. We sat on the stairs, like college pals. His questions were more specific. I remember him asking whether we had been chanting communist party songs during our lectures at Renmin. I shook my head in disbelief.

It is easy to see why a western reporter would automatically assume that an African journalist whose bills were being picked up by the Chinese government would be inclined to *transform* into a Chinese puppet. Whoever pays the piper dictates the tune. Except it is a narrow, unimaginative way to grasp the actual reality. Were there some of my colleagues who lapped up whatever propaganda was thrown our way? Maybe. But there were many others who fought through the fog, who disagreed with officials, who refused to publish anything that crossed their conscience. They didn't cower. They stood tall.

★

In December, I packed my bags.

And returned home.

You described leaving for China as going to war.

I thought it was a funny metaphor. Now I know it's true. ✛

ABOUT THE AUTHOR

Solomon Elusoji is a journalist. His first novel, about mental health and guns, will be published in 2020. He lives in Lagos.